LIVE C  ⌐OUD!

LIVING A PASSIONATE LIFE ON PURPOSE

Erika Larsson

AUTHOR OF WINNING IN BUSINESS, AND RISING HIGHER

Copyright ©2019 by Erika Larsson

LIVE OUT LOUD! *Living a Passionate Life on Purpose*

All Rights Reserved. No part of this book may be reproduced, stored in a retrieval system or transmitted by any other means without the written permission of the author, except in the case of brief passages embodied in critical reviews and articles where the author, title and ISBN are mentioned.

Published in the United States by:

Kindle Direct Publishing, North Charleston, SC

Printed in the United States of America

ISBN: 978-0-9983727-1-6
Library of Congress Control Number: 2017909589

The personality descriptor terms Supporter, Promoter, Planner, and Thinker are part of the Live Out Loud Personality System™ which can only be used with permission from Erika Larsson.

You can find information on Erika Larsson's training seminars, speaking, blog, and books at:

www.ErikaLarsson.com
admin@ErikaLarsson.com

Cover Design by Ann Crary of www.SeeItPrinted.com
Book Layout by Ann Crary of www.SeeItPrinted.com
Edited by Judy & Keith Hook and Katherine Sciarrotta

DEDICATION

With heartfelt gratitude, I dedicate this book to my daughter, Terrianne, and my husband, Mark. Thank you for believing in me, encouraging me, and supporting me to win. Thank you for reminding me, in moments of doubt, that I'm doing the work I was gifted and meant to do.

Through communication, acceptance of one another's unique gifts, and granting each other permission to be ourselves, we have created something magical together; a depth of love and respect that few ever experience. You've helped prepare me to teach others how they can have their most incredible relationships yet, rich in understanding and respect; for that, I thank you both!

ACKNOWLEDGMENTS

I feel incredibly blessed to have the support of my daughter, Terrianne, and my husband, Mark. They truly are the wind beneath my wings, providing support every step of the way as I pursue my passions and goals. Without them, my books and training seminars would not have come to fruition.

I attribute the knowledge I share in this book to those who pioneered and carried the personality-style temperament work forward.

Thanks to all the people who have provided an opportunity for personal growth in my life; especially my family, friends, former coaches, and bosses. I look forward to giving back to the world by teaching people how to transform relationships, improve communication, and reduce stress. My goal and desire are to see everyone living a life of passion, purpose, and joy!

I acknowledge my readers for picking up this book. Life Is about relationships and working on being the best version of ourselves. I'm thrilled that you want to learn how to live your life out loud and be, unapologetically who you were designed to be.

Last, but not least, a big thank you to God who has gifted me to encourage, inspire, motivate and lead. Apart from Him, I can do nothing!

Dedication 3

Acknowledgments 4

Contents

Part I   **Introduction**

          Introduction 9

Part II   **Understanding the Four Personality Styles**

Chapter 1   History of Personality Temperaments 11

Chapter 2   Everyone Is Uniquely Gifted 13

Chapter 3   Are You an Introvert or Extrovert? 15

Chapter 4   Identifying Your Personality Style 18

Part III   **Decoding the Four Personality Styles**

Chapter 5   Meet the Supporter Personality Style 24

Chapter 6   Meet the Promoter Personality Style 42

Chapter 7   Meet the Planner Personality Style 60

Chapter 8   Meet the Thinker Personality Style 77

Part IV   **Effective Communication with the Four
                Personality Styles**

Chapter 9   Effective Communication with the
               Supporter Personality Style 96

Chapter 10   Effective Communication with the
              Promoter Personality Style 102

Chapter 11   Effective Communication with the
              Planner Personality Style 107

Chapter 12   Effective Communication with the
              Thinker Personality Style 113

Part V   The Four Personality Styles at Work

Chapter 13   Appreciating the Supporter at Work 119

Chapter 14   Appreciating the Promoter at Work 123

Chapter 15   Appreciating the Planner at Work 128

Chapter 16   Appreciating the Thinker at Work 133

Part VI   Living a Purposeful Life

Chapter 17   Passion Is the Compass to Your Purpose 140

Chapter 18   Discovering Your Purpose 143

Part VII   Showing Kindness

Chapter 19   Making A Difference 146

Part VIII   Reflection

Chapter 20   You Are Uniquely Designed 150

Chapter 21   Ways to Live Out Loud 152

About the Author 153

Seminars and Testimonials 154

Erika's Books 156

References 158

PART I

Introduction

"The thing that is really hard, and really amazing, is giving up on being perfect and beginning the work of becoming yourself."
Anna Quindlen

INTRODUCTION

Is your life filled with purpose, passion, and joy?

Most people would be quick to agree that they desire healthy relationships and excellent communication with the people in their lives. But frequently, we can feel unheard, frustrated or misunderstood. Our attempts to gain understanding in conversations may seemingly fall on deaf ears; as people may not connect to our style or we misconnect to theirs. Communication battles inevitably breed stress, which has a negative impact on all areas of our lives; taking a toll on our performances at work, socially and at home.

When I learned about the different personality styles discussed in this book, it had a positive and profound effect on my personal and professional life. It was the first time ever that I felt like I belonged; like I was normal, and like my big dreams made sense. This is why I'm passionate about helping people figure out who they are, what they're most gifted at doing, and what their purpose is as well. Once we are able to do these three things, we can openly design and live the lives we were meant to live, without guilt, apology or a need to please others.

Everything at work, and at home, with bosses, clients, family, and friends, revolves around relationships. In this world connecting well is crucial. Therefore, it deserves our utmost attention. No personality style is better than the other; but they are clearly different. Learning to see and embrace our differences, helps us appreciate the contributions others can bring to our lives. By learning each personality style's strengths, we welcome a better life all around, one of acceptance and less judgment. Understanding people improves communications and connections in meaningful ways. This is what people crave today, but rarely find.

You are gifted with everything you need to live a life of passion, purpose, and joy! Thank you for allowing me to use my gifts to encourage, inspire and motivate you to be all you can be. I feel honored that you have picked up my book and are willing to learn and grow. From here on in, may all your relationships be rich in understanding, acceptance, and respect.

PART II

Understanding the Four Personality Styles

"Always be yourself, express yourself,
have faith in yourself, do not go out and look for
a successful personality and duplicate it."
Bruce Lee

Chapter 1

History of
Personality Temperaments

Mankind, in an attempt to fully understand human behavior, had categorized people into four main personality styles as far back as 370 BC, when Hippocrates created one of the very first systems recorded. Numerous personality systems exist today; designed by experts such as Jung, Meyers-Briggs, Keirsey, Lowry, Miscisin, and many others. They all share the same basic information but use different names for the four personality styles. I will spare you the details regarding the various systems, other than the one I designed called the "Live Out Loud Personality System™." This system uses names that are self-explanatory and easy to remember.

COMPARISON OF PERSONALITY TEMPERAMENT SYSTEMS

Live Out Loud Personality System™ Erika Larsson (the 2000's)	Supporter	Promoter	Planner	Thinker
Mary Miscisin (the 2000's)	Connector	Mover	Planner	Thinker
Don Lowry (the 1970's)	Blue	Orange	Gold	Green
David Keirsey (the 1970's)	Idealist NF	Artisan SF	Guardian SJ	Rational NT
Myers-Briggs (the 1950's)	ENFJ INFJ ENFP INFP	ESFP ISFP ESTP ISTP	ESTJ ISTJ ESFJ ISFJ	ENTJ INTJ ENTP INTP
Carl Jung (the 1920's)	Feeling	Intuition	Sensing	Thinking
Hippocrates (370 BC)	Yellow Bile	Blood	Black Bile	Phlegm

CHAPTER 2

EVERYONE is UNiQUELY GifTED

Everyone is unique and gifted! We are so complex that no one in the entire world is an exact duplicate of anyone else, not even identical twins. So, are we typecasting and putting people in a box by stating that there are only four personality styles? The reason we use this human behavior model is because for centuries it has been proven to be a simple, worthwhile method of identifying, and understanding mankind's behaviors.

We should always keep in mind that many variances come into play when we identify someone's personality style. Even though someone may have the same personality style as another and their style ranking scores may be identical; their similarities and differences, and how they respond to a situation may completely differ. People's behavior, is largely shaped by the way they were raised and the past experiences they have had. Both contribute to the person they become. Some are skilled at using their gifts more than others; some are introverted, while others are extroverted. All variables play a major role in what makes each of us a unique, one-of-a-kind individual.

Thinking that our personality style is superior to others is prideful. No style is better than another. We are all here for a purpose, and from birth have been gifted with natural abilities and talents. With ease we employ these gifts, experiencing creativity and joy when doing so. Our natural abilities continue to develop with use; eventually making us an expert in the areas we are gifted. Once we recognize our differences, we can work together, enrolling the gifts of others when we face a task that drains us - this is how powerful teams are built.

People are primarily dominant in one of the four styles, meaning that they have a natural way of behaving that is built into their DNA. We learn to differentiate each style by their unique gifts; how they process, behave, and function in the various scenarios of life. Being able to identify the most dominant characteristics helps us to begin the process of understanding ourselves and makes it easier to distinguish the similarities and differences of other styles as well. By learning what the four styles' attributes, needs, and stress inducers are, we begin to appreciate and accept their uniqueness, which is the first step to creating meaningful relationships.

The quickest way to discern a dominant gift is by how effortless the gift is performed. When a gift is in action, it is accompanied by a flow of energy and creativity. As a matter of fact, we could spend countless hours performing any dominant gift without tiring out.

Accessing this knowledge can help chart our course with confidence, and steer us towards doing what we were created to do. Understanding the differences and the contributions each style can make, is powerful information that will improve our personal effectiveness in all areas of life.

CHAPTER 3

ARE YOU AN
INTROVERT OR EXTROVERT?

According to renowned psychologist Carl Jung, credited as pioneering the terms "extroversion" and "introversion," there are two mutually exclusive attitudes, which children in their early years display with accuracy. Their preference for extroversion or introversion prevail throughout adulthood. The only time this may change is under extreme stress and unusual circumstances. The simplest way to understand the differences between extroverts and introverts, is to see whether someone generates and maintains their energy outwardly or inwardly. Extroverts are energized more by the external world and introverts are energized by their internal world.

The extrovert is most concerned with the world of objects, other people, and with how they impact the world. They are socially active, and most are well-informed about events taking place in their surroundings. They like to join groups, communities, and activities where they can easily interact with others. Introverts, on the other hand, prefer being by themselves. They enjoy alone time, with their thoughts and feelings, seeing the world in terms of how it connects to them. They think deeply and get energized and refreshed in quiet and solitude.

It is important to note that there are varying degrees of introversion and extroversion, depending on a person's state of mind, experiences, and phase of life. We all think, feel, sense, and experience the world in many different ways. Remember whether you are an extrovert or introvert, everyone is hardwired a certain way with characteristics that dictate how they gather their energy. We are all born with these preferences, and there is no right or wrong way to be.

It is much easier to determine the dominant personality style of an extrovert than it is an introvert, because extroverts share their dominant style with the world. Introverts use their dominant personality traits to process more internally, and typically communicate and behave in manners more indicative of their second style when interacting with the outside world.

With maturity, we can develop a flexible approach to our personality style, allowing us to choose the right attitude (extrovert/introvert) that fits in context to the situation or problem we are facing. This balance gives us freedom to be more of what we want to be, warding off a lot of unnecessary stress and wasted time.

The following characteristics are generally true for most extroverts:

EXTROVERTS

- Direct their focus and attention outwardly
- Are outgoing and energized by being with others
- Take in information through their five senses and focus on the here and now
- Focus on people and things
- Actively engage with their surroundings
- Speak and act readily without much reflection
- Like a flexible and spontaneous approach to life
- Naturally initiate conversations and interactions
- Like to participate in activities or situations that involve lots of people
- Have a breadth of interests and often have many friends
- Need to live and experience it to understand it

The following characteristics are generally true for most introverts:

INTROVERTS

- Direct their focus and attention inward
- Are energized by their inner world of ideas and impressions
- Have a hard time in large groups; too much interaction or small talk drains them
- Tend to make decisions based primarily on logic and objective analysis
- Recharge their batteries with solitude and solitary activities
- Focus on concepts and ideas
- Only participate verbally, when they have something to say
- Keep their social circle limited
- Prefer experiences with select individuals they are familiar or close to
- Tend to prefer depth of interest to quantity
- Need to understand it before they live it

CHAPTER 4

IDENTIFYING YOUR PERSONALITY STYLE

PERSONALITY STYLE WORD SORT

Rate how the words in the following columns describe your personality, by entering your scores in the boxes next to each word.

1 Point:	Least like me
2 Points:	Less like me
3 Points:	More like me
4 Points:	Most like me

To double check your personality style lineup, go to www.ErikaLarsson.com and take the free assessment.

Column A		Column B		Column C		Column D	
Peacemaker		Likes change		Prepared		Intellectual	
Accepts others		Bold and daring		Detail focused		Objective	
Supportive		Outgoing		On time		Likes to read	
Caring		High energy		Goal driven		Questioning	
Affectionate		Likes to talk		Traditional		Knowledgeable	
Likes helping		Risk-taker		Practical		Logical	
Patient		Quick to act		Organized		Problem solver	
Emotional		Playful and fun		Dependable		Likes technology	
Empathetic		Competitive		Responsible		Precise grammar	
Intuitive		Opportunistic		Likes routines		Innovative	
Good listener		Negotiator		Planner		Likes to fix things	
Spiritual		Straightforward		Hard working		Analytical	
Creative		Spontaneous		Loyal		Unemotional	
Nurturing		Freedom seeker		Follows rules		Private	
Avoids conflict		Multi-tasker		Efficient		Competent	
Total		**Total**		**Total**		**Total**	

Add up your scores for each column. Also, enter your totals in the Discovering Your Personality Style section below. Next, complete the Personality Style Ranking Lineup, using its directions.

DISCOVERING YOUR PERSONALITY STYLE

Insert your scores below for each column:

_____ Column A Score – SUPPORTER

_____ Column B Score – PROMOTER

_____ Column C Score – PLANNER

_____ Column D Score – THINKER

PERSONALITY STYLE RANKING LINEUP

Enter your personality style names in order of dominance below:

_____ highest score - Dominant Style

_____ 2nd highest score – Secondary Backup Style

_____ 3rd highest score – Third Style

_____ lowest score - Challenging Style

It is helpful to commit your style lineup to memory. We function mostly from our Dominant and Secondary Backup styles.

LIVE OUT PERSONALITY SYSTEM™ TERMS

Terms used to describe the four personality styles in this book are:

Supporter: Nurture and care for people

Promoter: Bring action and fun to the world

Planner: Work bees who get things done

Thinker: Change agents who improve the status quo

Every style is excellent in its own right. Our challenge is to recognize our differences, honoring each style's gifts and the contributions they make in life.

HOW YOUR PERSONALITY LINEUP AFFECTS YOUR ACTIONS

Dominant Style

Your primary, most dominant style is what guides and directs you through life's experiences. The attributes of your dominant style are part of your DNA. You were born with these gifts; using them is as natural as breathing; they take little thought or effort to perform.

Secondary Backup Style

Your secondary backup or "go-to" personality style is the co-pilot that supports the actions of your most dominant style. Most people operate between their top two dominant styles most of the time. If you are an introvert, chances are you display this side of your personality to the public and use your dominant style inwardly in your alone time.

Third Style

You will access the traits of your third personality style when situations demand it. If your third style's score is close to your second, these traits will be more apparent, allowing you to access them with more strength.

Challenging Style

Your fourth rated style is often challenging. This is significant because the traits are the least natural to you. Chances are they are also the characteristics you least appreciate or understand, and therefore can cause you to criticize others who possess them. Your fourth personality style offers the most opportunity for growth.

DISCERNING YOUR PERSONALITY STYLE

Sorting out the perfect order of your personal characteristics may take some time. As you get more familiar with the traits for all four personality temperaments, you may discover more strength in a particular style than you had originally scored. Often traits of a parent were demanded of you. Therefore, you adapted these traits to survive in life, and they are now second nature, making it harder to evaluate your own natural gifts. The easiest way to reach clarity is to look at the gifts of each style, asking yourself if you are energized and happy when you carry them out or is it just a learned trait.

We all have characteristics from all four of the styles in varying amounts. Many personality experts agree, "Thinkers" are the most likely to report an equal spread of personality characteristics. Their keen ability to analyze helps them activate their brains to produce examples of circumstances in which they have used each trait. Once they continue their research and examine which traits energize them, and which they perform with less zest, they quickly determine that the majority of their preferences fit into the Thinker style. It's a typical process for the Thinker to question and to examine everything from all angles, but in the end, their analyses produce reliable results.

Understanding our own personality traits and what makes our style tick is a good start. Becoming proficient at identifying the styles of others comes with observation and practice. With a little training, you can skillfully discern the personality temperament of everyone you meet, with speed and accuracy, enhancing your relationships with those around you.

Everyone is gifted! Embracing our differences removes much of the stress in our day-to-day dealings with other styles.

PART III

Decoding the Four Personality Styles

"Embrace who you are and don't make
any apologies for being yourself."
PictureQuotes.com

Chapter 5

Meet the Supporter Personality Style

Supporters are polite, friendly, and helpful. They love people and devote time to connecting with others; talking and listening, sharing feelings and profound truths. They are the least judgmental and most inclusive of all the personality styles, readily able to see different points of view, providing empathy and respect for individuality.

Their feelings can be easily hurt and when criticized, they have a hard time not taking it personally. They are emotional and wear their hearts on their sleeves, often crying with someone who is hurting or laughing with those who are happy. They will establish good eye contact, and make others feel cared for and comfortable.

Because they are perceptive and gifted with intuition, they read between the lines quickly, discerning false motives or intentions, even when no one is speaking. They instinctively know when a person is dishonest and when a person has unexpressed needs. Their perceptive nature helps them understand, accept and care for people more than any of the other personality styles and it's why they make excellent counselors.

Supporters are highly creative and have great imaginations. They are always seeking to understand the human race. Most are deeply spiritual and spend lots of time developing their inner self to gain understanding about their path and purpose in life.

They have to be careful not to become a real dumping ground for other people's problems. Giving too much empathy can cause them a sense of emotional heaviness, making it difficult for them to let go of sadness or concern they feel for others. If they are not careful, they will take on the problems of others as their own, which can result in depression. On the other hand, whenever a Supporter can provide useful insights, advice, and counseling they feel energized, fulfilled and happy. They do best by learning to create healthy boundaries with people.

Supporters are optimists. They see the good in everyone and will give people who hurt them chance after chance. Their support of others is unending. They are the wind beneath the wings of those leading the way and will assist in any way they can with necessary tasks. Coming to the aid of those who display a need, makes a Supporter feel fulfilled.

Emotional tension or the venting of hostility makes them extremely uncomfortable. Supporters are lovers, not fighters. They dislike conflict and will go to great lengths to foster harmony, cooperation, and togetherness. They prefer to walk away from a fight instead of engaging in it, both at home and in the workplace.

Supporters are nurturers and caregivers who possess a deep emotional attachment to their loved ones. Creating memories with their family and friends gives them a sense of purpose and great joy. Their loyalty and devotion to the people in their lives are second to none. They are the glue that holds relationships, organizations, and families together. Whatever they can do to make others feel good, they enjoy doing.

This quadrant of people is at peace, appreciating everything and everybody, and is contagiously enthusiastic. They like interacting with others and behave with honesty and integrity, always encouraging those who doubt themselves. You can ask them a question and expect to get a truthful answer.

They have lots of compassion for people and animals. Often, they will get involved in humanitarian or animal rescue projects and will come to the aid of anyone hurting. They can commonly be found helping individuals that are ill, disabled, disenfranchised, or otherwise in need. They help the helpless, adopt pets from the animal shelter and will support any cause that has affected them personally. They are tolerant, kind, and generous to those who display a need, be it in the physical, spiritual or emotional realm.

Supporters need meaning in their lives and feel special when others show appreciation for their authenticity and unique contribution. They focus on making a difference in the world, and their quest to do so is never-ending.

They prefer not to lead and enjoy being part of a team where they can inspire others and cheer for them. They are outwardly receptive and non-judgmental and sense the exact moment when people need nurturing, complimenting or validation. They are cooperative rather than competitive, and because they get along with others, they make excellent mediators.

Supporters have no need for power or control. Instead, they thoughtfully dedicate much of their time to helping others feel good about themselves. Helping others gives them a lot of peace and joy, and it's what fills them up. Hospitality is part of their DNA; they like cooking and entertaining, making it easy for guests to feel welcome in their home.

Most Supporters love nature and the outdoors. Nature is life to them, and they prefer to head out to the trails, mountains, and wilderness rather than spending time in the bustling city.

Supporters value personal growth and strive to balance mind, body, and emotions. To this end, they often populate self-help, bodywork, or human potential seminars, and often seek a career path in one of these areas. Supporters gravitate towards careers in alternative or complementary medicine such as homeopathy, massage, naturopathy, etc. Many opt to work as counselors, psychologists, nurses or in areas where they can help people, animals or the environment. Some express themselves in creative or fine arts careers like; music, drama, writing, painting, sculpting, graphic arts, or architecture to name a few. They are highly represented among journalists as they excel in both the written and spoken word.

Money is not as important to a Supporter as it is to the other three personality styles. It is seen as a tool to achieve ideals rather than a way to gain power, status, or win the admiration of other people. They are best described as "earthy," both in appearance and lifestyle. They are typically health conscious and seek alternative health advice outside the standard medical system, even if it means they have to pay for it themselves. Often, they garden and grow organic food. They like natural products, shampoos, cleaning supplies, etc., and may spend a lot of time at the health food store. They recycle, do their part to take care of the planet and get involved in causes that create positive change.

Supporters tend to collect keepsakes, mementos, souvenirs, and clothing that are meaningful to them. It is not unusual to discover their graduation, bridesmaid, or wedding dress tucked away in the closet or an item that a loved one gave them. They are very reluctant and unwilling to part with anything that has fond memories.

Because relationships mean more to them than things, they are often content with simple living arrangements, second-hand furniture, and décor. Extravagant meals, vacations or wardrobes are rarely high on their list of priorities.

Supporters wrote the book on romance and love giving affection, caring gestures, a hug or pat on the back. They may write poetry for their loved one and will always remember special occasions. They thrive when they feel loved and accepted and will bend backwards to ensure their relationships remain stable and intact. They have a phenomenal ability to love people unconditionally.

In their interactions with people, Supporters have the capacity to look beyond the immediate surface to see the real truth. They look for the good in people which often results in a romanticized view of others. They are known to stay in unhealthy relationships, hoping the person will eventually change for them. Their optimism and patience with people can also work in their favor, helping to create lasting relationships that thrive.

Supporters are very authentic and build relationships by sharing personal information from their heart. You can count on them being genuine, passionate and real in all their encounters. They generally have lots of friends, and most likely will keep their friends for life. They regard life as something to share, feel and experience with people. They desire to understand others and be understood.

Supporters have a sensitive nature and avoid mean, negative, or obnoxious people at all costs. They excel at motivating, encouraging and inspiring others to be their best. They are in the world to minimize conflict, be peacemakers, lovers, and supporters, giving hugs to all who need them, and a listening ear to a troubled heart. Their dedication is to make a difference in the world by helping others see their full potential.

A SUPPORTER'S GIFTS AND TALENTS

All of us are here to use our gifts to make a contribution to the world. A dominant Supporter's gifts are a natural part of their DNA, making them effortless to use. Most of their gifts involve nurturing, creating, helping or supporting, which is their primary purpose in life.

They are passionate and represent love, harmony, and relationships. When Supporters are allowed to express their unique gifts, it contributes to their overall success and happiness.

- Fostering relationships
- Acknowledging others
- Caretaking
- Optimism
- Teaching and training
- Mercy and compassion
- Hospitality
- Empathy
- Nurturing
- Kind and considerate
- Encouraging
- Giving
- Sympathy
- Peacemaking
- Enthusiasm
- Helping and serving
- Supporting
- Affectionate - hugs
- Imagination and creativity
- Spiritual insights

- Intuition
- Listening
- Mentoring
- Communicating
- Patience and tolerance
- Motivating
- Recruiting
- Romance
- Sensitivity
- Connecting with others

JOYS

Supporters gain satisfaction, fulfillment and joy from the following:

- Affection and loving gestures
- Performing and fine arts
- Social acceptance
- Activities that promote unity and teamwork
- Using their imaginations
- Events that inspire them
- Personal relationships and friendships
- Plays and movies that are emotional
- Entertaining family and friends
- Being a positive influence in situations
- Nature and things pleasing to the eye
- Self-development, growth, and spirituality
- Love and romance
- Meaningful conversations
- Being creative
- Helping others

VALUES

Values are an inner guide that directs a Supporter's actions and gives their life purpose and meaning.

CORE VALUE: Relationships

- Compassion
- Long-lasting friendships
- Peace and harmony
- Tolerance
- Honesty and integrity
- Intimacy and affection
- Nature
- Kindness
- Human potential – seeing the possibilities in others

- Self-actualization
- Spirituality
- Helping to meet the needs of others
- Sensitivity
- Creativity
- Patience
- Connection
- Communication, sharing, interaction

NEEDS

Meeting a Supporter's needs is a sure way to gain their cooperation. Their comfort, health, happiness, and success, depends on satisfying these requirements through continued opportunities and experiences. When their needs are not satisfied, frustration and stress increase, which often leads to conflict; or worse, emotional or physical health problems.

- To be accepted, well-liked, understood, and included
- To live in peace and harmony
- Honest and sincere communication
- Freedom from control
- Appreciation and acknowledgment
- To be self-expressed, real, and personal; sharing thoughts and feelings
- To live a meaningful life of purpose; making a difference
- Conflict resolution
- To act in agreement with others to ensure no one is hurt, offended, or left out
- To affirm others and be affirmed
- Interaction with others
- To feel needed
- Love, romance, affection, and intimacy
- Relationships – family and friendships
- To cultivate potential in self and others
- To contribute; nurture, support, and care for the needs of others
- To use imagination and creativity
- To feel unique and special

STRESSORS

A Supporter's capacity to succeed in life is significantly diminished when they experience the following:

- Lying and cheating
- Controlling or aggressive people
- Insensitivity and insincerity
- Disharmony and conflict
- Isolation and being ignored
- Lack of communication
- Negative, arrogant, and rude people
- Lack of appreciation
- Having to say "No" to requests
- Being compared, talked about or criticized
- Lack of physical contact and affection
- Cruelty to people or animals
- Lack of individual expression
- Budgeting and financial planning
- People who lack warmth and caring
- Rushed timelines
- Being yelled at or spoken to in a harsh tone
- Tunnel vision without being open to new possibilities

REACTION TO STRESS

When Supporters are stressed out or overwhelmed, their personalities fade and their attributes quickly do an about-face and become their challenge. In this state, they often display attention-getting misbehavior and may even tell a lie to save face. They cry easily and appear depressed and withdrawn. Many will express their frustrations and emotions by yelling, screaming or using anger in hopes of gaining back control. All they need to return to their caring state and get back on track is a little reassurance, support, and love.

When experiencing low self-esteem or stress, they may behave in the following ways:

- Lie to "save face"
- Quit caring
- Play victim - wallows in self-pity
- Harbor resentment
- Disguise feelings with a false happy face
- Blame others, not taking accountability
- Dramatize events – using words like "always" or "never"
- Withdraw - spending time daydreaming and fantasizing
- Eat comfort food to soothe their wounded feelings
- Emotional outbursts – yelling, crying or exploding with anger
- Takes everything personally – become overly sensitive
- Control by giving the silent treatment
- Display rigid and uncooperative attitudes
- Become judgmental, or gossipy
- Become overly involved in helping others to avoid their own feelings
- Passive-aggressive
- Sabotage opportunities and relationships
- Social withdrawal from everyone close to them
- Serious mood, body language is unfriendly and closed off

CHALLENGING AREAS

Every personality type has areas that challenge them. The Supporter personality style is especially fearful of stepping out of their comfort zone to make changes or speak their mind because they fear they will upset someone. They do everything possible to avoid conflict and keep peace and harmony in their environment.

With consistent practice, the challenging areas for the Supporter personality style become easier to deploy.

AREA OF CHALLENGE	NEED TO PRACTICE
Self-validation, saying, "I matter!"	Taking time to refuel by pampering themselves.
Accepting criticism without reacting negatively.	Discerning between positive and negative criticism accepting that certain criticism can help them improve and is not an attack on their character.
Wanting to escape conflict or disharmony.	Allowing disagreements. Using accountability language (I feel, I think, etc.) to dispel anger and work on reaching a win/win resolution.
Worrying and taking on the problems of the world.	Letting others grow and learn from their problems without feeling compelled to help them.
Making things sound better/worse than they are.	Eliminating "drama King or Queen" behavior.
Asking for help, especially when feeling overwhelmed.	Making requests and accepting help when it is offered.
Making decisions without getting approval first.	Acting without agreement from others.
Trying to please everyone.	Accepting that they can't please everyone.

AREA OF CHALLENGE	NEED TO PRACTICE
Lack of planning. Supports others but don't make plans or goals of their own.	Setting goals and making their life and what they want a priority.
Going without. Suppressing their feelings and what they want to the point of depression.	Expressing feelings. Self-expression through dance, music, art, writing, etc. can also help.
Initiating activities or action for fear of failure or rejection.	Initiating activities and making decisions without anyone's approval because it's something they want to do.
Budgeting - spending money on others instead of saving for things like retirement.	Financial accountability. Hiring a financial planner to help make a solid financial plan that includes activities and retirement and sticking to the plan!
Being assertive, taking a stand and speaking up when they have opinions, wants, and needs.	Saying, "I matter!" My opinions, needs, and wants are important. Stating what they want to win the respect of others.
Sacrificing honesty for harmony or withholding unpleasant information to avoid hurting another's feelings.	Avoiding lies to save face - realizing they are not responsible for another's feelings.
Dealing with details, instead of ignoring them.	Enrolling people who can help with the details.
Disciplining children or staff, especially if they have to fire an employee.	Leadership. Doing what they know is right without guilt.

AREA OF CHALLENGE	NEED TO PRACTICE
Ignoring their own needs to help others who request their help.	Not allowing others to project guilt or use emotions to get their way. Doing one thing a week for themselves that they want to do (i.e.: fishing, massage, reading, walking, etc.)
Rescuing or being an enabler. Wanting to fix problems for others.	Holding people accountable without being an enabler. Selectively choosing the issues they take on.
Saying "YES" to everything they are asked to do.	Saying, "NO!" and being okay if others disapprove.
Being a doormat and being used by others.	Setting healthy boundaries.

TURN TO SUPPORTERS FOR

Supporters will lend a helping hand whenever they are asked to. They are great at creating unity and bring their support and optimism to tasks that involve their gifts.

Hospitality – Their door is always open, and they like having people drop in and stay for a chat, a meal or overnight. A Supporter's passion and focus are to make people feel welcomed, doing what it takes to help them feel safe, comfortable and included. No one will be alone when a Supporter is around. They make great greeters for any function. At work, they are great at helping newcomers get oriented.

Acceptance – Supporters value relationships and provide a tremendous amount of understanding, tolerance, patience, and mercy towards everyone they meet. Accepting, praising, encouraging and validating others, is as natural as breathing for Supporters.

Mediation – They enjoy harmony and therefore exert effort to dispel any conflicts at home and work. They don't like to take sides in any dispute; instead, they will listen to everyone involved, fostering collaboration to reach an agreement, and ensure peace has returned. Their intuition guides them in the process, and because people sense that they are heard and cared about, they usually cooperate.

Personal and Spiritual Growth – Most Supporters are very spiritual, and it's rare to meet an atheist. They claim to feel connected with a power greater than themselves and believe in God or a higher power. Supporters spend lots of time searching for the meaning and purpose of their existence and claim to find the answers in their chosen faith. Many attend church and most pray. They are proponents of personal growth and love the journey of learning, growing and living their full potential.

Encouragement and Cheering Up – Supporters are cheerful and optimistic, gifted at seeing the best in both people and situations. They provide comfort and understanding and help others see the silver lining. Because they love to grow and learn from every circumstance life presents, they can encourage others to do the same. They use their caring, intuitive, and creative ways to lift spirits, in particular for those who feel downtrodden or sad. They are quick to give genuine compliments.

Friendship – Since Supporters value relationships above all else, they love connecting with others. As friends, they consistently listen, care, nurture, support, and encourage the people in their lives. They are super intuitive and know what to say and when to say it. They know how to comfort, and they know how to motivate people to be their best selves. You can count on a Supporter friend to be there for you when you need them.

Support – Supporters are excellent at supporting others to win. When you want a team cheerleader or someone to come alongside to lend a hand, involve a Supporter.

Guidance to Make Change – Supporters understand people better than anyone else and are experts at knowing how a change will impact the people involved. Because change often takes people out of their comfort zone, it's good to involve a Supporter as they understand what is needed to keep everyone calm and engaged, ensuring the transition from old to new will be smooth. They make great counselors as they have the ability to guide people to welcome change.

Teaching and Mentorship – Supporters are patient and love to guide others to reach their potential. They feel rewarded when others are inspired and motivated by what they teach. As a mentor, they know when to push their student and when to pull back, always keeping the pupil's needs in mind as they develop and learn. Their discernment about people allows them to adapt their teaching style, giving each student the attention, they need to learn best.

Teamwork – They are excellent team players and great followers. They are sensitive to the needs of others and are happy to roll up their sleeves and do what is necessary to reach the goal. They cheer everyone on and encourage team members to do their best, giving compliments that inspire and motivate them. They are masters at reading people and do what it takes to ensure they have a cohesive team.

Creativity and Imagination – If you want to brainstorm ideas and create training in the areas of service, morale building, team-building, communication or people skills, make sure you include Supporters. They have great imaginations that will help spark new original ideas as well as inspire everyone involved to contribute their innovative ideas. They are also very gifted at being craftsmen. Because of their artistic flair, many express themselves through writing, music, art, acting, decorating, building or making things. They are never short on ideas on how to make something beautiful.

Contribution to a Cause – Any cause or charitable organization that contributes to the well-being of people or animals will tug at the heart strings of Supporters. They love making a difference and don't mind volunteering their time or financial support to such a cause. They are quick to support organizations that provide humanitarian or animal rescue and help.

Event Design – Supporters love creating and are perfect candidates for developing an event, be it a wedding, a company party, or a family function. Their imagination and creative flair will help make the event a success. They take everyone's personality into account when they plan. A perfect combination would be to let the Supporter handle the parts of the function that requires creativity and have a Planner personality style, handle the logistical and budgetary details.

Help – Supporters love lending a hand, and when they can contribute to lightening the load, it energizes them. When asked to help, they will rarely say no. They are the wind beneath the wings of leaders. Supporters are the people who always show up to do work; no job is too small for them. When they contribute to others, they feel included, wanted and needed. They are the ones that help their friends move or bring a meal to someone who is sick.

Inspiration and Motivation – Supporters have a built-in gift of inspiring and motivating others. They especially love using these traits to help people reach their true potential in any area of life. In a work situation, they are a true asset to any team, as they know just what to say and do to inspire and motivate those around them.

Romance Ideas – No one understands love and romance better than Supporters. They could author several books on the topic. They love being in love, and showing romantic gestures is second nature. If you want to impress your romantic interest, take advice from a love pro, the Supporter.

Peacemaking – Harmony is super important to Supporters. They will help dispel any conflict to create a peaceful, harmonious atmosphere or relationship.

A LISTENING EAR – When you need to vent, a Supporter will be your confidante, providing active listening for as long as you need it. They are the least judgmental of all four personality styles and are gifted listeners, often without saying a word. They are patient, discerning and compassionate, and have the ability to understand and share the feelings of others without discrimination.

HOW SUPPORTERS ARE VIEWED BY SELF AND OTHERS

Supporters view their behavior as well-meaning, loving, helpful and supportive. Others may not see their behavior in the same positive light, which is upsetting for a Supporter and challenging for them to accept and understand, given their sensitive nature and commitment to helping others.

Usually, a judgmental perception about a person's personality characteristics comes from people who least understand them; whose personality style lineup scores are the lowest in their category. Creating harmonious relationships involves looking through different lenses to understand our personality differences. Holding positive perceptions of others, by realizing how gifted they are, contributes to everyone's success.

PERCEIVES SELF AS	OTHERS MAY PERCEIVE THEM AS
Self-expressed and personal with people, sharing who they are and how they feel.	Too emotional or personal when conversing, quick to shed tears.
Optimistic, considerate and trusting, believes people are inherently good and gives them chance after chance to prove themselves.	Naïve, too trusting, easily persuaded or duped. Attracts people who use and abuse them. Lets others "walk all over them."

PERCEIVES SELF AS	OTHERS MAY PERCEIVE THEM AS
Romantic - believes in love. Wants to show their affection with all kinds of meaningful gestures like touching and hugs.	Overly sentimental and mushy, adds meaning and significance to every romantic gesture. Smothering, too touchy-feely.
Genuinely interested in the welfare of others, enjoys nurturing and having others depend on them. Compelled to help when someone has a need.	Codependent tendencies - takes care of the needs of others, without taking care of their personal needs. Overbearing with their help.
Flexible and cooperative - goes with the flow to create harmony and peace.	Says "yes" when they should say "no." Says "sorry" too much. People pleasers.
Affirming, considerate of other people's feelings, needs and wants when making a decision. Doesn't want anyone upset.	Indecisive, slow to make decisions without input from others. Overly dependent on external approval. Co-dependent.
Works hard for any cause they support.	Gets used by others, for having a bleeding heart.
Excellent communicator. Puts people at ease – goal is to get to know others so they can meet their needs, inspire, and motivate them to be their best.	Nosey, asks too many personal questions, talks too much. Their prying is intrusive. Comes off as "busybodies."
Spiritual, always searching for deeper meaning and purpose in life. Believes in a higher power. The promoter of personal growth and spirituality.	Embraces out-of-the-norm spiritual practices, flaky, easily persuaded, irrational. Should keep their beliefs to themselves and leave others alone.
Pleasant, warm and friendly. Priority is to get along with everyone and show people they are valuable.	Tender-hearted, too soft, too nice, too giving.

PERCEIVES SELF AS	OTHERS MAY PERCEIVE THEM AS
Polite and pleasant – make their needs known in a non-confrontational manner - doesn't make requests or demands to avoid conflict.	Weak. Manipulative - drops hints about their desires and pouts when people don't do what they want. Passive-aggressive tendencies.
Compassionate, sympathetic, and empathetic towards all living things. Knows when others need help and will go to great lengths to provide it.	Overly sensitive and sympathetic, compelled to rescue all living things. Should mind their own business until someone requests help.
Unselfish, supportive and sincere in all their actions. Gives to everyone who needs help. Likes to please people and go the extra mile.	Rescuer, enabler, over-reactive. Emotionally moved by pity. They allow people to take advantage of them.
Sensitive and caring. Uses intuition to interpret what is said, or unsaid, especially when criticized. Considerate – tries to see all sides of an issue.	Dramatic. Fragile – oversensitive and emotional - misinterprets words and intentions. Takes everything personally and gets hurt feelings.

CHAPTER 6

MEET THE PROMOTER
PERSONALITY STYLE

Promoters are optimistic, have a light-hearted attitude towards life, a great sense of humor and are playful. It's a lot of fun to spend time with them. They love to laugh and remind us all not to take life too seriously. To them, life is to be enjoyed at every opportunity, viewing activities as a game to win. They are very independent and have lots of friends, interests, and hobbies.

They are extremely friendly, charming, and social, and have the ability to talk to anyone with ease, moving from one topic to another in conversation. Promoters tell the best jokes and keep the atmosphere happy, light, and entertained. If they don't laugh several times in a day, there is something wrong. They are great showmen who love sharing anecdotes and testimonials. They enjoy being the center of attention, not necessarily seeking it. However, they bask in it when it occurs.

Promoters possess natural childlike qualities and a certain innocence that others often find refreshing. They get over unpleasant setbacks quickly, and in a short time they forgive and move on. They are not afraid to let their inner child out to play and often come bouncing into a room announcing their presence. They bring energy, fun, and entertainment to all their social interactions. Most will tell you they don't want to grow up or grow old. They continue to be free spirits into their old age refusing to be confined or held back.

Their exceptional insight into people allows them to assess them instantly and mirror their body language and emotions to establish an immediate rapport. With their promoting nature, they promptly capture the attention of the public. They are very expressive and can entertain a crowd without effort, spontaneously sharing their entertaining stories. Promoters enjoy sharing interpersonal feelings and having deep conversations; your secrets are safe with them.

They catch on fast and act on and implement new ideas without missing a beat. Promoters don't like to practice; instead, they prefer to learn with a hands-on activity. They will spend hours perfecting an activity or skill, having a good time on the way to improvement. Because Promoters process information the moment they receive it, they find it difficult conversing with people who pause to think before they speak.

Promoters are happy people. They are active and outgoing. They can express themselves in a variety of ways which doesn't always appeal to every personality style; however, most people, in general, love their pleasant company.

They adapt well to new experiences and thrive on the unpredictable which is why the excitement of traveling is one of their favorite things to do – preferably first-class. They love to spend money and are by nature very generous and extravagant, giving expensive gifts to the people they care about, rarely paying attention to what is in their savings account.

Most personality styles don't like change, but Promoters love it and find it exhilarating. They lack fear and are risk-taking adventurers, who like movement, dancing, and physical activities. They like participating and living life to the fullest. Many pursue competitive sports or frequent a gym to expend some of their energy. If you want to bungee jump, skydive, ride a roller coaster or any other risky adventure, ask a Promoter to join you as they get a rush from these activities, and usually won't say no.

Like the Thinkers, Promoters love music, and many are highly skilled in this arena. Due to their artistic pursuits, most popular song artists, and entertainers are likely Promoter dominant personality styles. Some are so naturally talented in music that spending hours practicing like the Thinker style would is not necessary. Instead, they play when they feel the urge, taking pleasure in the countless hours they spend concentrating on their performance until they reach contentment. Their endurance level passes that of the other styles when they are focused. Because they naturally tend to focus on solutions, they can endure physical suffering, hardship, hunger, and fatigue in a way that other styles cannot. This stamina, along with their stubborn minds gets them through the most grueling of challenges.

Physical activity and motion help Promoters release emotional upsets, anger and bottled up energy, helping them to feel invigorated, bright and ready for action again. Promoters love the challenge of competing, and their goal is to place first in any activity. Their energy, self-esteem, and confidence are at an all-time high when they conquer and win a challenge.

Their antidote to avoid boredom is to keep busy and stay in action. Promoters constantly hunger for new experiences that will stimulate their five senses – new sights, smells, sounds, tastes, and touch. To gain their cooperation, tell them a story, use testimonials or concrete, practical examples when you talk to them.

Like the Thinkers, Promoters can also see the "big picture." They are visionaries, capable of seeing possibilities that others do not. Promoters are quick-thinking and accustomed to probing until they uncover new ideas. They are innovative when it comes to producing results, and they swiftly seize opportunities when they discover them.

Promoters dream "big" and have "big" goals, however, they rarely write them down. They are always making the right connections that will help bring their goals to fruition. They see the goal in their mind's eye and instead of creating detailed plans, prefer to figure things out as they go, changing course when needed. They like trying new things and are capable of creating whatever they think up. They are usually the ones that bring a fresh perspective or a new edge to an old idea to make it a hit. Because they read people well, they instinctively know what appeals to the masses, and this is what they seek to deliver.

Even though Promoters are not great at dealing with details, they have an excellent memory for detail and with ease can recall what occurred on a particular date, what someone was wearing at an event or describe every detail of the hotel room they stayed at last month. Promoters never forget the date or time of an upcoming event they want to attend; however, most struggle with remembering the mundane things like where they left their car keys, sunglasses, wallets, purses or what they were supposed to bring to the company barbecue.

They process information out loud and when they have a problem, they need to talk about it. More words come out of their mouths than any of the other personality styles. They have frankness of speech and can come across as blunt, speaking what is on their minds without giving much thought to how others may perceive what they say. They mean no harm; they are honest and dislike playing emotional games. What you see is what you get with a Promoter. If they offend anyone or hurt their feelings unintentionally, they apologize at once and make it right.

The great thing about a Promoter personality is that they don't sit and wallow in self-pity or hang onto hurt or anger. Instead, they let go quickly and move on to their next adventure. Even with life's setbacks and unfortunate events, Promoters typically adapt much faster than other personality styles, believing that everything happens for a reason and always works out in the end.

Many Promoters may underperform in academic settings; not due to a lack of ability, but to a lack of stimulation and challenge. Because they rapidly take in information, they get drained and 'check out' when forced to deal with abstractions or theories for too long. This explains why more Promoters than any other personality style, are apt to be diagnosed with ADD or ADHD. Because of their social prowess, they often distract other children in school rather than focus on their work. It is not uncommon for remarks to appear on their school report cards stating that they interrupt and talk too much in class. They are most productive in informal environments, especially when they can move about.

Promoters have a natural eye for beauty, style, and aesthetics and are concerned about keeping up their appearance. They are edgy, with a tasteful, flamboyant way of dressing and decorating their homes, and are never intimidated by loud colors or trendy styles. They keep up with current trends and fashions and are not afraid to try a new hair color or the latest fashion-forward hairstyle. They help to stimulate the economy because they buy what they like, without concern for cost. They are generous hosts, and their homes are always open to visitors.

They appreciate excellent food and know the best restaurants in town. They know where all the entertainment venues are and many like to frequent live theater. In their garage, you will find power tools, maybe a bicycle, a vintage or luxury sports car along with all types of sports and outdoor paraphernalia.

Promoters are the entrepreneurs of the world. They are unafraid of trying new things, blazing new trails with great zest and enthusiasm. They are swift on their feet, highly creative and multi-talented. They do well in a variety of careers, especially ones that involve action, movement, risk-taking, flexibility, creativity, and freedom of expression. They work well under pressure and can think on their feet. Careers in sports, fashion, hosting a TV show, acting, music, dance, sales or marketing are a sampling of what appeals to them. Others may work in construction, as firemen, pilots, negotiators, or mechanics, etc.

Even though they are restless and easily distracted, they can focus well when partaking in discussions and activities that are stimulating. Life is an adventure for Promoters. They like freedom and movement. They want to do what they want when they want, without having to answer to anyone or being confined by limitations and obligations. They are daredevils who release their excess energy through physical activities and action. Having challenges and the freedom to act is what makes them peek-performers.

A PROMOTER'S GIFTS AND TALENTS

All of us are here to use our gifts to make a contribution to the world. A dominant Promoter's gifts are a natural part of their DNA, making them effortless to use. Most of their gifts involve action, adventure, promotion, and entertainment, which is their primary purpose in life.

They are energetic and represent fun, freedom, power, persuasion and swift action. When Promoters are allowed to express their unique gifts, it contributes to their overall success and happiness.

- Optimism and enthusiasm
- Adventurous nature
- Bravery and boldness
- Motivation
- Competitiveness
- Problem solving
- Creativity
- Resourcefulness
- Dealing with crisis
- Using tools
- Direct communicator
- Efficiency
- Quick to act
- Networking
- Flexibility
- Generosity
- Proficiency
- Humor and playfulness
- Leadership
- Lighthearted nature
- Change
- Multitasking
- Confidence
- Negotiating
- Opportunistic
- Adapting
- Persuasion
- Energy and endurance
- Resilience
- Engaging
- Risk-taking
- Self-expression
- Generating ideas
- Spontaneity
- Influencing and promoting
- Troubleshooting
- Decisiveness
- Visionary

JOYS

Promoters gain satisfaction, fulfillment, and joy from the following:

- Adventures and activities
- Being generous
- Performing
- Being recognized for individual success
- Competing and being the best
- Excitement and fun
- Moving their body or dancing
- Coping with problems and crisis
- Putting plans into action
- Taking risks
- Troubleshooting
- Choice and variety
- Being in charge or leading
- Freedom
- Attention
- Personal indulgences
- Using tool

VALUES

Values are an inner guide that directs a Promoter's actions and gives their life purpose and meaning.

CORE VALUE: Freedom

- Instinct for opportunity
- Action
- Adventure
- Change and variety
- Challenge
- Hands-on experiences
- Risk-taking and being bold
- Competition and winning
- Physical activities
- Flexibility
- Humor, excitement, and fun
- Individual achievement and rewards
- Spontaneity
- Creativity and aesthetics
- Productivity – getting things done immediately
- Forthrightness

NEEDS

Meeting a Promoter's needs is a sure way to gain their cooperation. Their comfort, health, happiness, and success, depends on satisfying these needs through continued opportunities and experiences. When their needs are not satisfied, frustration and stress increase, which often leads to conflict; or worse, emotional or physical health problems.

- Independence and freedom to do as they like
- Direct communication – no game playing
- To talk and express themselves; sharing stories, jokes, and experiences
- To be noticed and shown attention
- To seize opportunities; act on a moment's notice; be productive and make things happen
- Humor and playfulness
- Immediate feedback; straightforward answers
- Informal environment

- Physical movement and mobility
- To be skillful; have mastery of tools and hands-on activities
- To receive recognition for performance, skills, and ideas
- Involvement and social contact
- To engage in entertainment and fun
- To attain tangible rewards
- To network and be resourceful; meet needs
- To be spontaneous; be able to switch gears with little thought
- To negotiate; gain cooperation from others
- Challenge, competition, risk, boldness
- An adrenalin rush
- Variety and options to choose from
- Flexibility and change

STRESSORS

A Promoter's capacity to succeed in life is significantly diminished when they experience the following:

- Lack of freedom or choices
- Inflexibility; especially with time
- Unchallenging activities
- Lack of humor and play
- Repetition and unnecessary routine
- Inactivity and waiting
- Rules and regulations that bog them down
- Paperwork, being stuck at a desk
- Inability to negotiate or change outcome
- Feeling trapped or bored
- Lack of money and resources
- Not being allowed to talk or participate
- Criticism, negativity, nagging
- Indecisiveness
- Reading instructional manuals
- Lack of physical movement

- Being told what to do or how to do it
- Slow people
- Rigidity

REACTION TO STRESS

When Promoters are overwhelmed from stress their personalities no longer sparkle, and their positive attributes quickly fade. In this state, they often break the rules, act rude, and display anger, lying or cheating behavior. To return to their fun-loving state and get back on track, they need someone to encourage them to take action, move forward, and get out of their current environment to experience something new. They are quick to recover but sometimes need a little push to move forward.

When experiencing low self-esteem or stress, they may behave in the following ways:

- Overcommit and under deliver
- Display lying and cheating behavior
- Unrestrained and noisy behavior
- Act, or speak before considering consequences
- Blame, point fingers to faults of others
- Sarcastic, hurtful, mocking of others
- Stubborn, demanding of their way
- Look for an escape and will quit, drop out or detach, not caring if they burn a bridge
- Defiant or rude outbursts
- Purposely break rules
- Demonstrate anger and aggressive behavior
- Use manipulation to get what they want
- Avoids taking action, due to boredom
- Use avoidance behavior
- Seek immediate gratification or quick fix of outside stimulants
- Reject advice

- Seek escape from reality by daydreaming
- Impulsive – moves from one thing to another without completing anything

CHALLENGING AREAS

Every personality type has areas that challenge them. A challenge for the Promoter personality style is structure, rules or anything that restricts their freedom to move, take action or express themselves. They will break all rules to secure their freedom.

With consistent practice, the challenging areas for the Promoter personality style become easier to deploy.

AREA OF CHALLENGE	NEED TO PRACTICE
Bureaucracy, structure, and restrictions; rules, and regulations, policies and procedures.	Obeying rules. Accepting that structure and regulations are in place for a reason.
Completion - starting things without follow-through.	Discipline to follow through to completion, or enrolling others gifted in this area to help.
Acting or speaking on impulse.	Taking time to think before speaking Or acting.
Boredom from predictability or sameness at work or in relationships.	Being the game changer instead of wasting time daydreaming about it being different.

AREA OF CHALLENGE	NEED TO PRACTICE
Impatient, especially when they have to wait.	Patience. Directing energy in a positive direction when they have to wait for something.
Too much information, data or instructions.	Asking for it in an abbreviated version or bullet-point format.
Being told what to do.	Letting people know that they can make requests, not tell them what to do.
Situations void of humor or fun.	Accepting that everything isn't always fun or humorous.
Being on a roller coaster of having lots of money or being broke.	Saving for a rainy day so there is money for entertainment.
Car problems or technology issues.	Servicing everything regularly and keeping track of when certain maintenance is required.
Being stuck at a desk pushing paper.	Taking frequent breaks and moving around.
Facing disapproval or criticism. Ego-sensitive.	Getting ego out of the way and learning how to accept constructive criticism and input.

AREA OF CHALLENGE	NEED TO PRACTICE
Too many details.	Paying attention to required details.
Reading "how-to" manuals or instructions.	Enrolling someone to read the instructions, while they perform the hands-on application.
Silence or sitting still.	Being quiet, still, and relaxed.
Getting antsy from lack of physical movement.	Getting physical movement frequently and exercising regularly.
Exaggerating to make things sound larger than life or more appealing.	Sticking to the facts without embellishing them to make the story more exciting.
People who are slow in their actions, movements, speech, or thinking.	Learning to appreciate other personality styles that process differently and need more time.
Being on time or having to be somewhere at a precise time.	Being punctual and respecting other people's timelines.
Deadlines and schedules with no flexibility.	Planning ahead to meet deadlines.

TURN TO PROMOTERS FOR

Promoters love being asked to contribute their ideas. They will happily bring their energy and enthusiasm when you involve them to help in the areas they are gifted.

IdEAS ANd INSPIRATION – Promoters are playful and like to brainstorm ideas. Their creative brains act as idea machines, spewing new ideas out at a rapid rate. They get excited when asked to contribute their thoughts and can quickly generate fun suggestions for family gatherings, conferences or any event. When they are excited, their enthusiasm and optimism inspire everyone around them.

LEAdERShip – Promoters are confident leaders. Put them into any situation, with little experience, and they'll make it work. Their innovative brains figure things out as they go, producing top results every time. They think out of the box and are not afraid to take a risk and try new things.

GETTING ThINGS DONE ImmEdIATEly – Promoters are all about seizing the opportunity and taking immediate action. They do well with sudden change and can switch directions at the turn of a dime. They are optimistic, innovative and gifted at finding shortcuts. When you want things done quickly, ask a Promoter.

RESOURCEfulNESS – They are social, love small talk and networking. Promoters have a massive database of connections and people to draw from. If they don't have an immediate answer, they know someone who knows someone else who has the resource you need. They are very outgoing and interactive, building relationships wherever they go.

ProblEM-solvING - As natural-born trouble-shooters, they remain calm during a crisis. When there is a problem, they immediately jump into solution mode. They are independent and make quick decisions. They have a knack for harnessing talents in others, delegating tasks as necessary to keep everything under control. No one can generate ideas and solutions faster than a Promoter.

Skillful Use of Tools – They are hands-on people who have the ability to accurately build and create things that provide a more pleasant life for others. They may be a creative workshop leader, an award-winning hair stylist, a recognized artist, the builder of notable buildings or even cities. They perform their cutting-edge ideas with ease and precision.

Motivation – Their excitement is contagious, and they use their charm to motivate people to participate with them. They have a knack for enrolling everyone in their vision, inspiring them to take action when required. They are confident, and people want to do what they do.

Adventure and Entertainment – Their energy and optimism come through in their adventures and when they have the opportunity to entertain someone. Their sharing is usually in story form, filled with larger-than-life examples, and expressions that keep their audience entertained. Life is an adventure for a Promoter and they want to share it with you. If there is an event, enroll their participation and they will ensure it is a memorable one.

Fun and Laughter – Promoters are light-hearted, quick-witted and laugh more than any of the other personality styles. Their child-like character can even find the humor in the mundane and unpleasant. Because humor is part of their DNA, they cheer others up naturally. They love creating fun and laughter everywhere they go.

Negotiation – Gaining the cooperation of others and turning a "no" into a "yes" comes naturally for the Promoter personality style. Their creative minds will present a continuous stream of options necessary to reach their goal - rarely do they ever need to compromise.

Forthright Response – Promoters are straightforward and tell it like it is. They are not afraid to have an opinion, even when it is not a popular one; they give you their uncensored response with little concern about being politically correct.

Challenge – Motivated by their natural competitive nature and sense of fun they play full-out in any competition and play to win. A challenge keeps things interesting and gives them a chance to pull out all the stops with their innovative ideas. Their optimism helps keep things enjoyable.

Tasks Requiring Risk – Promoters are courageous and have no fear of taking risks. They make risky investments and like daring adventures like bungee jumping, fire walking, or skydiving. They are bold and fearless and often do things for the sheer enjoyment they get from the accompanying adrenaline rush. They feel alive when they test the limits.

Variety – Promoters get bored quickly and therefore create new and innovative ways of doing things to feed their voracious appetite for variety. Variety is the spice of life they say. They love to travel, experience new foods, adventures, fashion, etc., and will share their experiences, giving others who aren't quite as experimental some new options to try.

Recreation – Promoters like to be active, and they need to be in motion. They have a zest for life and are the first to try new things. They need to use up their physical energy and are therefore involved in several activities where they can push and exert themselves. Going to the gym, mountain bike riding or extreme sports, all appeal to a Promoter.

Promotion and Sales – They can promote and sell almost anything to anyone. When they believe in something, look out! Their enthusiasm and the way they present the possibilities persuades even the most difficult to convince. Top sales people in most companies are likely Promoters.

Spontaneity – Because they have no issues with change, they will drop what they are doing to participate without hesitation. They enjoy the stimulation, freedom, and the excitement of something new. If plans change, or they get a spur-of-the-moment invitation, they will optimistically go with the flow.

Generosity – Promoters are generous with their finances, time, energy, and ideas. They like to give extravagant gifts. Their creative minds like to give the unexpected and wrap it with artistic flair. They go beyond expectations in their job or extra-curricular activities.

HOW PROMOTERS ARE VIEWED BY SELF AND OTHERS

Promoters view their behavior as energetic, open, efficient and productive. Others may not see their behavior in the same positive light, which baffles a Promoter who lives to take action and make things happen.

Usually, a judgmental perception about a person's personality characteristics comes from people who least understand them; whose personality style lineup scores are the lowest in their category. Creating harmonious relationships involves looking through different lenses to understand our personality differences. Holding positive perceptions of others, by realizing how gifted they are, contributes to everyone's success.

PERCEIVES SELF AS	OTHERS MAY PERCEIVE THEM AS
Bold and assertive. Direct communicator, open, honest and real with a "tell it like-it-is" approach. Self-expressed and passionate in their dealings with others.	Obnoxious, pushy, rude and loud. Blunt delivery, doesn't think about their gestures or behaviors and how they will affect others. They speak before they think.
Has a playful attitude, easy-going, happy-go-lucky, and carefree. Likes to go with the flow and leave option open in case things change due to their many interests. Will make a commitment with the option to change their mind.	Irresponsible and flaky, changes mind at the last minute with no regard for their actions or subsequent consequences. Disregard for timelines and being on time. Disrespectful, indecisive and unreliable.
Relaxed, entertaining, fun-loving, enjoying life. Values the freedom to be self-expressive and likes to have choices. They are playful and like having fun. Capable - likes to compete and perform to get top results. Loves entertaining others.	Not serious, scattered and not able to stay focused or on task. Instead wastes time by goofing around and making jokes, putting more effort into having fun than into work. Carelessly lazy – very thoughtless.

PERCEIVES SELF AS	OTHERS MAY PERCEIVE THEM AS
Flexible, independent, self-fulfilled and carefree. Believes in living life to the fullest, always exploring new possibilities, welcoming new ideas and change. They are spontaneous and like to experience every thrill that presents itself.	Selfish and self-centered. Neglects duties and postpones responsibilities to suit their schedule with no regard to what others want. Lacks focus. Quickly goes from one thought to another, from one experience to another. Untrustworthy.
Action-oriented, proficient multi-tasker. Likes choices and flexibility and will often push limits to get things done quickly, their way.	Unfocused and scattered. Switches direction when it suits them. Bends rules to get what they want – always trying to beat the system.
Mover and shaker who makes things happen in record time. Efficient, eager and gifted at seeing where corners can be cut to save time. Quick to seize an opportunity and take action. Likes to compete and plays to win, even if it means breaking protocol now and then.	Takes unnecessary risks. Bypasses protocol and chain of command and forges ahead without getting permission to achieve what they want. They are impatient, demanding, and act in haste without thinking it through. Disrespect their bosses.
Multi-tasker who enjoys variety and change, able to switch gears and act at a moment's notice. Hands-on, very productive. Stimulated by variety and change.	Scatterbrained, unable to make a plan and stay on task. Cluttered and unorganized. Continues to work when people are trying to get their attention. Lacks focus and discipline.
Deals well with crisis and chaos. Clear-headed; makes quick decisions to solve the problem. Can see what needs doing and delegates tasks with ease. Can prioritize instantly.	Bossy and demanding. Uncontrollable - doesn't take the time to assess the situation before acting. Doesn't involve others who may have more knowledge. Flies by the seat of their pants.

PERCEIVES SELF AS	OTHERS MAY PERCEIVE THEM AS
Adventurous, courageous, risk-taker. Lives on the edge, with no regrets. Likes challenge and a real adrenaline rush.	Irresponsible and stupid. Doesn't consider consequences that could result from their actions. No consideration for safety.
Spontaneous and quick to think on their feet. Creative trouble-shooter. Confident that they can deal with anything that comes their way. Can easily switch gears.	Unprepared - creates last minute stress for others by not being ready on time. Wings it instead of preparing a solid plan ahead of time. Not serious about anything.
Successful with a 'fake-it-till-you-make-it' motto. Will act the part until the goal is accomplished and will improvise along the way until they get it right.	Disrespectful, dishonest, and phony. Inconsiderate, a real slacker that has no solid goals. Smooth talkers.
Does not like to be boxed in with rules and regulations. After all, rules are made to be broken. Freedom seeker.	Disobeys rules - acts as though they don't apply to them. Takes shortcuts, ignoring the applicable regulations and restrictions. Disrespectful.
Friendly, adaptable and outgoing. Enjoys the process of building rapport. Expert networker who is very resourceful.	Always has an agenda. Wastes time by talking and telling stories, putting more effort into socializing than into work. Uses others for personal gain.
Clever, confident and self-assured leader with superior negotiating skills. Optimistic and innovative problem solver who thinks outside the box, able to see possibilities that others don't see. Able to inspire and motivate others to embrace their point of view.	Controls and manipulates to get their way. Untrustworthy, will stretch or minimize the truth, cheat or lie to get what they want or to accomplish their goal. Their motives are self-serving and can't be trusted.

Chapter 7

Meet the Planner Personality Style

Planners are among the most disciplined of all four personality types. They are self-motivated and results-oriented. If they have a goal in mind, nothing will stand in their way. They are the ones who sign up for a gym pass and attend on a regular basis. They are the people who set a goal to lose ten pounds and accomplish it. They are the worker bees that bring projects to realization. They are incredibly productive and love the feeling they get from accomplishing things. Getting results energizes them to take on more duties and responsibilities.

Planners like familiar routine and appreciate knowing what to expect. The more often they do something in a particular way; the more likely they are to adopt the pattern. Often, they will eat a certain type of meal every day for breakfast or lunch, without entertaining a change. If something works, they stick with it. They have the most difficult time of all four personality styles with change. They prefer things that work stay the same. They rely heavily on past precedent, both behaviorally and when relating to ideas. Once they have established a routine, they don't want it changed or discontinued.

Typically, Planners are relatively serious and offer little in the arena of spontaneity or humor. That doesn't mean they can't have fun, but for the most part, the fun has to be scheduled. They are reserved and take longer to warm up to people and can sometimes be viewed as cold, bossy, stubborn, inflexible, or nitpicky, but are more easygoing than people credit them for being. They may also appear unfriendly and uninterested, and that is because they always have a planned agenda to tend to, they want people to "cut to the chase" as time is valuable to them. Once their tasks are handled, they will make time for you.

Planners are loyal to their friends and partners and gravitate towards people who embrace a similar lifestyle and world view. Despite their outer confidence and imposing presence, they are often inwardly insecure and not sure of themselves. They are the most judgmental of all four personality styles, which is mainly due to their lack of internal control. A Planner experiences anxiety when they sense that they are not in control, hence their propensity for restlessness and hypervigilance.

Being on time is critical for the Planner personality style. As a matter of fact, they are the ones that show up ten minutes early for an appointment. They do not like it when others are late and expect their friends and co-workers to show up at the agreed-upon time. They especially get irritated at the Promoter personality types who are frequently late. Planners expect scheduled meetings to start as scheduled as they dislike wasting time, no matter what the excuse is.

The Planner personality style is a stickler for service. They give exceptional service and expect the same in return. They will get annoyed with retail clerks who ignore them and will not hesitate to file a complaint to the person in charge whenever their experience is less than excellent. Their purpose for doing so is to help others improve the service they provide.

They are driven and have a long list of things to accomplish, often appearing rushed or unapproachable due to their focus. When they are focused, they only want to give time to the things on their list. When they are busy, they may not listen well if you interrupt them, especially to small talk. They are very direct in their communication and want to get straight to the point.

Relaxing is difficult for a Planner because there is always work to do. They schedule relaxation and play time with activities that are structured, organized and well-planned. To Planners, there is a right and wrong way to do everything, including how to play games. They are rule-bound and will be quick to point out violations or errors when participating in any games and expect everyone to adhere to the rules if they are to play.

Planners strive to be their word and practice what they preach. They are steadfast in all their commitments. They value security and save money for their children's education and their future needs. They know what their bank account balance is at any given time and will always stick to their budget. They only make a purchase when it's necessary and planned, and will look for the best deal, buying items on sale whenever possible.

Because Planners are self-sufficient and responsible, they frown at those who take advantage of other people's generosity, labeling them as freeloaders or takers. They want to be the providers, not the receivers, of service or charity. Should they ever accept a helping hand; they will be quick to devise a plan to repay their provider. Staying debt-free is a high priority.

Structure and safety are huge values for Planners. They take these seriously and will labor tirelessly to ensure they are intact both at home and work. They will set plans in place should there be an earthquake, flood, or emergency; ensuring that everyone knows their precise role and what to do if any of these events occur. Safety also includes being financially prepared for emergencies and retirement.

Social status is often a high priority for Planners. Although tight-fisted with their money, they will spend money on a nice car and home. They like quality and will purchase items that have longevity; they will save, until they can afford to buy whatever they want. As far as their dress goes, they are conservative and prefer to invest in classic clothing that they can wear for years to come.

They like everything to be consistent and predictable in their lives and feel best in an orderly and stable environment. Their homes are clean, neat and tidy. These people have a place for everything, and everything is in its place. They are master organizers who gain energy every time they check off an item on their 'to-do' list. Getting things done takes priority over play.

Planners are sticklers for manners! They know proper etiquette and have high expectations in this area. They are very appropriate for everything they do and like to keep things professional, especially in any dealings they have with people outside their home environment. They are very determined and reliable, but may appear domineering, and demanding when their focus is interrupted.

A Planner will bring order to chaos, staying calm and unemotional while focusing on a practical solution. They are detailed, dutiful, and realistic. They will consider the facts before they reach a conclusion and can be counted on to get the job done right.

Another attribute the Planner personality style possesses is accountability. They are ethical, honest, and conscientious. They do what they say they will do and can always be depended on for accuracy and following through to make responsible decisions.

They plan ahead for trips, packing a few weeks in advance. If they are going away, they will book the hotel months ahead of time to get the best deal. They start making a list of what needs to be done immediately after a decision to do something is made and continually review and add new items to it, making sure nothing is left out.

Planners gravitate towards careers that are structured and predictable, positions where they act as guardians, such as management positions, legal positions (police), financial planners, teachers, or political positions. Many work in business, banking, service occupations, military or civil service. Because social standing is important to them, they prefer to associate with prominent people and established, recognized institutions.

Planners defend as well as preserve traditions and conventions, especially familiar ones. Commonly they will carry on traditions that they grew up with, including sticking with their childhood religion and they will continue to pass these beliefs and customs on to their family. They value family time and run an organized and planned lifestyle, ensuring they allocate time for family activities and friendships.

Planners respect their elders and honor the chain of command in the family and other areas of life. They teach their children responsibility from a young age, and chores are assigned early on. No child of theirs will ever be lazy, nor will they ever depend on others to pay their way. They teach their children that they must do their part as one's status must be earned.

Planners are self-disciplined and responsible and can be counted on to do their duty. They ensure that what others create is implemented, with everything running smoothly. They organize everything, provide directives, ensure rules are adhered to, and help people to be accountable, doing what they are supposed to do. They are efficient and meticulous, providing detailed plans that help bring completion to projects. They are dependable; the worker bees that stay committed and focused on finishing the job.

A PLANNER'S GIFTS AND TALENTS

All of us are here to use our gifts to make a contribution to the world. A dominant Planner's gifts are a natural part of their DNA, making them effortless to use. Most of their gifts involve preserving, enforcing, or doing something, which is their primary purpose in life.

They are loyal and represent duty, responsibility, and guidance. When Planners are allowed to express their unique gifts, it contributes to their overall success and happiness.

- Following directions
- Providing safety and security
- Being practical
- Etiquette
- Bringing order to chaos
- Structure and routine
- Dutiful and goal-oriented
- Dependability
- Loyal
- Detail-oriented nature
- Efficient and precise
- Enforcing rules, regulations, policies and procedures
- Accountability
- Family-oriented
- Commitment
- Law abiding
- Discipline
- Managing
- Organization – creating systems and order
- Saving time, money, or resources
- Preserving customs and traditions
- Scheduling

- Administration
- Providing sound judgment
- Planning
- Self-motivation
- Being punctual
- Responsible and reliable

- Realistic mindset
- Ethical
- Stability
- Completion
- Honesty
- Trustworthiness

JOYS

Planners gain satisfaction, fulfillment, and joy from the following:

- Security
- Being prepared
- Completion of tasks
- A sense of belonging
- Establishing routines
- Timelines
- Fairness
- Time for family

- Home
- Tradition and heritage
- Providing stability
- Reaching closure
- A sense of order
- Tangible rewards
- Doing the "right thing"
- Job satisfaction

VALUES

Values are an inner guide that directs a Planner's actions and gives their life purpose and meaning.

CORE VALUE: Responsibility

- Status
- Commitment
- Practical decisions and common sense
- Etiquette, formality, and Professionalism
- Accomplishment
- Standards

- Duty and responsibility
- Being on time
- Religious heritage
- Morality
- Family traditions
- Loyalty
- Honesty, and integrity
- Time and resources

- Order and organization
- Security, safety, and stability
- Routines
- Rules, policies and procedure

NEEDS

Meeting a Planner's needs is a sure way to gain their cooperation. Their comfort, health, happiness, and success, depends on satisfying these needs through continued opportunities and experiences. When their needs are not satisfied, frustration and stress increase, which often leads to conflict; or worse, emotional or physical health problems.

- To plan before engaging in activities
- Respect, appreciation, and acknowledgment
- To adhere to rules, regulations, policies, procedures, and laws
- A structured formal environment
- To show loyalty and commitment to family, friends, and employer
- Orderliness, organization, and cleanliness
- Safety, stability, and security
- To get results – get things done; check items off on their "to-do-list"
- To preserve tradition, heritage, and customs
- Proper etiquette - formal and professional
- To follow routine
- To be economic; save time, money, and resources
- To do the right thing
- Consistency – rely on the tried and true
- Reliability and accuracy
- Honest communication
- To be punctual
- Clearly defined boundaries, roles, requirements, expectations, and timelines
- To attain closure and completion
- To be realistic and practical

STRESSORS

A Planner's capacity to succeed in life is significantly diminished when they experience the following:

- Carrying most of the responsibilities
- Being surprised
- Taking risks
- Time pressure – being rushed
- Lack of control
- Incomplete tasks or conversations
- No savings account
- Unnecessary or unplanned change
- Too many things going on at the same time
- People who are late
- Indecisiveness
- Disorganization and chaos
- Interruptions
- Waste of time, money or resources
- Not knowing what the plan is
- Having to be spontaneous
- Irresponsibility
- Procrastination
- Unfulfilled expectations or dishonesty
- People who don't follow through

REACTION TO STRESS

When Planners are overwhelmed or feel pressure, their personalities can be a challenge to face. Their good traits quickly disappear as they try to regain their footing. In this state they often complain and behave with self-pity, blaming others for their problems. They exhibit anxiety and worry, and their judgment of self and others can become quite malicious. They become bossy in an attempt to gain back control of their environment. To help a Planner recover this loss of power, encourage them to take the time to reach clarity about what needs to happen. Pointing out their value and reminding them that they are important will help them move forward.

When experiencing low self-esteem or stress, they may behave in the following ways:

- Being domineering and bossy, "I know better than you" attitude
- Displaying a pessimistic outlook
- Judgmental of self and others
- Self-righteous, right about everything
- Impatient
- Arrogant - insensitivity to feelings
- Short tempered
- Stubborn, rigid and inflexible
- Resistant to change
- Exhibits anxiety and worry
- Fatigued and depressed
- Blame others for the stress they feel
- Gossip about others when they are angry at them
- Tattletales, pointing out others' wrongs
- Verbally aggressive, short and blunt in their communication
- Black and white thinking
- Threatening and demanding
- Complain and feel sorry for themselves

CHALLENGING AREAS

Every personality type has areas that challenge them. Nonconformists seem to be a major challenge for the Planner personality style. They feel that everything runs better with rules and regulations and feel it's their obligation to ensure these mandates get enforced. Duty runs their life so as not to be labeled as lazy or irresponsible.

With consistent practice, the challenging areas for the Planner personality style become easier to deploy.

AREA OF CHALLENGE	NEED TO PRACTICE
Finding balance. Duty and task take priority over everything else.	Relaxing with no agenda. Making a plan that incorporates all areas of life, including time to relax.
Worrying, being anxious and letting go.	Trusting that everything will work out without their control.
Finger wagging and stopping the use of "Should" and "Shouldn't."	Allowing and accepting that people have a choice to do things their way.
Perfectionism. Need to realize that their high standards can be discourage-ing to others.	Accepting the standards of others and living by example rather than making others wrong.
Controlling and micro-managing others.	Accepting that other people are capable.
Spontaneity.	Being spontaneous without pre-planning things.
Listening to others and validating what they say.	Listening skills. Letting others talk without interrupting them or finishing their sentences.
Responding, without judgment, to the feelings of others.	Being non-judgmental.
Following.	Realizing that other people can be competent leaders too.

AREA OF CHALLENGE	NEED TO PRACTICE
Having flexibility instead of being so rigid when it comes to changing course or doing something differently.	Being flexible and open-minded about going a new direction. Being open to receiving input from others.
Playtime instead of always being focused on their 'to do' list.	Lightening up and setting aside their serious side for some unscheduled fun.
Being pessimistic, always looking for all the reasons why things won't work.	Being optimistic, looking for why it will work.
Being self-righteous or being a tattletale. Judging people who have differing standards and values.	Accepting people for who they are, what they do, and how they process. Going directly to the source they have an issue with to rectify the matter.
Doing everything themselves to ensure it is done right.	Allowing others to share in the responsibilities. Accepting that There are different standards.
Thinking they know the only way to get a job done or produce results.	Accepting that there is more than one way to do a job to get desired results.
Change.	Accepting that change is inevitable and good.
Being bossy.	Not bossing people around – being a team player.

AREA OF CHALLENGE	NEED TO PRACTICE
Being overly loyal to a company, thinking they won't survive without them.	Believing that other people are just as capable as they are.
Creating win/win situations.	Working to create a win/win situation with people rather than an "I'm right" and "you're wrong," which is a win/lose.
Acting like they are the authority on everything. Telling people what to do and how to do it.	Treating people with respect. Making requests rather than demands.

TURN TO A PLANNER FOR

Planners like to belong and provide service. They like being in charge and can be counted on to use their gift of organization to create the structure for any project they are asked to undertake.

Administration – They are professional in every sense and know proper etiquette in business and at home, having high standards in these regions. They steer others towards the accomplishment of goals and directives by planning, organizing and supervising others.

Service – Planners are great in service-type organizations to identify tasks that are incomplete, using available resources to get the job done. The services they provide are more task-focused than people-focused.

Tradition, Heritage, and History – They like things to remain the same and therefore hold their heritage in high regard. At home, they continue traditions from their childhood and do their utmost to preserve their family history. They are devoted and loyal to family, friends and their place of work.

They also work at maintaining the culture and traditions of the country they live in, the place they work, and any service groups where they have a membership.

Doing Things Right – Be it manners or the correct way to do something, a Planner is usually well-informed. They believe there is a right and wrong way for most everything. They are self-disciplined, and independent, taking pride in knowing what is appropriate and traditional while doing things the right way.

Planning Events or Projects – They are gifted at knowing what needs doing and will create a step-by-step plan to ensure the event or project is completed correctly and on time. When planning an event, working with a Supporter can be a great combination, as long as they stay away from the creative planning and focus on the logistics and budgetary needs. They are great at making practical decisions and setting realistic timelines for completion.

Teaching – Planners like to instruct others in a systematic way and will follow the rules of the curriculum to ensure their pupils get the full training they deserve. They enjoy it when others advance in their knowledge on the subjects they teach.

Responsibility and Duty – They are independent, self-disciplined, dependable and reliable. Planners get energized by results; they like to be busy and thrive on having a full plate of "to-do's." They work hard and gain great pleasure from setting goals and executing them with excellence. They always do what they say they will do and can be counted on to deliver results in a timely fashion.

Management – Planners can be put in charge of a vision or project and will make a detailed plan to include all the necessary steps required to bring the project to fruition. They manage all aspects of a project by providing direction to others, ensuring the plan is accomplished with accuracy.

Organization – Planners value order and are masters at establishing systems that contribute to things working better; be it a system for your goals, files, time, or things. You can put a Planner in utter chaos and they will straighten it out, being happy doing it. They keep things neat and tidy.

Saving Time and Money – Planners are always punctual. Because time is valuable to them, they are masters at using it wisely. When there is work to do they won't be sitting around chatting about life; instead, they will have their nose buried in the task at hand. Planners are security conscious and when it comes to money and budgets, they like to save; knowing how to cut corners and delighting in coming in under budget with money to spare. To save time or money in any situation, Planners can help. They are frugal and know where to find a bargain.

Details – They are gifted at taking a complicated project or task and breaking it down into a detailed step-by-step process. Their brains work in such a way that they can speculate all the necessary elements required to complete the tasks, without missing any steps. They cross the "T's" and dot the "I's" leaving no detail unattended.

Honesty – Planners are ethical, trustworthy and confidential. They like truth and rarely tell a lie. They dislike gossip and negative talk about others and are loyal to those they respect. You can ask them a question and you'll get a straight, honest answer. At work, they are trusted with financial information and budgets.

Policy, Procedures, and Rules – They like to know what the policies, procedures, and rules are so they can be compliant with them. They are law abiding in all areas. They are often instrumental in the design and implementation of policies, procedures, and rules, especially if they are non-existent.

Accuracy – Planners are perfectionists and like everything completed correctly. Because they are sticklers for detail, they will ensure they check and double-check their work to ensure its accuracy. They don't like guessing and like to base everything on fact. They make great proofreaders and can keep track of cash or a budget with precision. Rarely will they make an error.

Scheduling – Planners live their lives on a timetable. They plan everything, and as a result, they always have a "to-do" list on the go. They accomplish a lot because of their organized scheduling of tasks and events. If they have something scheduled, you can count on them to show up or get the job done. They are clock watchers, because to them every minute counts.

Fairness – As long as everyone follows the rules, they are usually very reasonable. They have a sense of justice and will pay careful attention to what is just and impartial. In situations that need discipline, they will consider all the facts before imparting what the correct action should be to remedy the problem.

Creating Routine and Structure – Planners thrive on the predictable and hence, love structure and routine. At home, they usually get up at the same time every day and follow the same routine they've had for years. At work, they will be on time and will have regular, systematic methods for completing their daily duties. When a new routine needs to be created and implemented, a Planner will handle it like a pro.

Direct to the Point Communication – Planners don't want to spend a lot of time talking about the task or project because they want to get to doing it instead. Because they value time more than any of the four personality styles, they prefer getting to the point in a conversation. They are very direct when they speak and have little need for connecting on a personal level when there is a job to be done.

HOW PLANNERS ARE VIEWED BY SELF AND OTHERS

Planners view their behavior as responsible, reliable and dependable. Others may not see their behavior in the same positive light, which baffles a Planner, especially since they believe their way is right.

Usually, a judgmental perception about a person's personality characteristics comes from people who least understand them; whose personality style lineup scores are the lowest in their category. Creating harmonious relationships involves looking through different lenses to understand our personality differences. Holding positive perceptions of others, by realizing how gifted they are, contributes to everyone's success.

PERCEIVES SELF AS	OTHERS MAY PERCEIVE THEM AS
Efficient and diligent; goal and task oriented. Makes detailed plans and executes them by strictly adhering to all the designed steps.	Uptight, scheduled, agenda driven. Judgmental of people who don't share their work ethics or method of doing things. Unbending and very opinionated.
Realistic, sensible, practical, knows the most efficient way to do things.	Resistant to change - likes to do things the way they've always done them. Lacks innovation and imagination. Stays in comfort zone.
Law-abiding. Follows the rules, regulations, policies and laws and ensures others do the same.	System-bound. Gullible – follows the rules without questioning them.
Organized and efficient, a place for everything and everything in its place. Orderly and neat with tasks, house, office, and dress.	Rigid and inflexible, close-minded about new ideas or routines. Judgmental of others with differing standards and views. Anal.
Reliable, trustworthy and credible. Provides structure and routine. Can navigate any plan using their great leadership and management skills.	Controlling and bossy - doesn't take other people's wishes, opinions or feelings into account. Self-righteous.
Knows what is appropriate, right or wrong, good or bad.	Opinionated, inflexible and domineering. Thinks their ideas and their ways are superior and right. Very judgmental and controlling. Tattle tails.
Traditional and stable with upright values.	Stubborn and uncompromising. Does a lot of finger wagging and finger pointing.

PERCEIVES SELF AS	OTHERS MAY PERCEIVE THEM AS
Dependable and decisive decision makers. Realistic views. Collects all the facts to make sound decisions.	Close minded, not open to new possibilities, prefers to stick to the tried and true even when presented with better suggestions.
Loyal to family, friends, and organization. Upholds traditions. Steadfast.	Predictable, old-fashioned values and traditions. Dull and boring. Not open to new possibilities.
Capable and well-planned. Good at taking charge and managing projects – knows what is required.	Anxious, worry-wart, afraid to think outside the box or take a risk. Won't deviate from plans or be open to suggested change.
Security-minded - disciplined with finances and saving for the future.	Frugal and cheap. Doesn't know how to enjoy life. Afraid to take risks.
Responsible and conscientious; stable and dependable. Ensures that chores and duties are completed before they play.	Serious, dull and boring; lacks enthusiasm, spontaneity, and fun.
Accountable, timely and efficient. Can be counted on to get the job done. Punctual - respects the time-lines of others.	Time-bound. Criticizes others who don't adhere to their strict time management style. Has to have an agenda for everything they do. No freedom. Lacks spontaneity.
Firm and persistent. Results-oriented.	Uncompromising and stubborn. Acts like they have authority, by raising their voice or yelling to get what they want. Bossy.

CHAPTER 8

MEET THE THINKER
PERSONALITY STYLE

Thinkers value intelligence and are usually well educated. They may not always have college or university degrees, but their ferocious appetites for learning ensure they stay well informed on topics of interest. They often received good grades in school, score high on IQ tests and may hold leadership roles as well.

Thinkers are known for their extensive vocabularies and impeccable grammar. They enjoy the written word and often prefer to express themselves fully and precisely through writing, because it gives them an outlet to sort through their thoughts and time to convey them completely.

Play rarely occurs to a Thinker. They have a tendency to take life seriously, using their inner logic to navigate and discern as they go. For them, work becomes play, especially acquiring knowledge that will carry their goals forward. That's not to say they don't know how to have fun! Thinkers love new experiences and will seek them out. In many cases, they enjoy extreme sports; like skiing black diamond runs, hiking Everest, or backpacking in a third world country.

When Thinkers go on vacation, they seek out different experiences from the norm; exploring new cultures, restaurants, ethnic foods or new sites while thoroughly enjoying the discoveries they make along the way. They enjoy travel and will know months ahead of time where they want to go, as their research is a big part of their fun and relaxation.

Thinkers are continuous learners. It is uncommon to find a Thinker without a library membership, a Kindle or a similar item giving quick access to the books they love. They are avid readers from a young age and always have several books on the go at once. Although they can access books electronically, they greatly prefer traditional books, rarely parting with the hundreds they acquire. Thinkers are the people who keep bookstores in business and will gladly spend a whole day combing their shelves.

Not only do they love books, but they also love technology. They will have the latest technological devices, know all their functions and can give you the reasons that their device is the best. They do their homework before making a purchase and are therefore an excellent resource for those who are not as technologically savvy.

Because their brains are wired to connect the dots, they are most often the very people who create modern technology, programs, apps, and games. When learning a new program or app, logically they will want to know each step of its function and why it functions the way it does – it's how they learn.

Many Thinkers are musically inclined, which is a wonderful outlet for energy and emotion. Most Thinkers enjoy music and have an extensive and varied collection of old and new tunes. They value a premium stereo which allows them to hear the lyrics and musical tones clearly. Music can become a comfortable way to be social for them, and many play in a symphony or band.

A high percentage of Thinkers are introverted, often feeling self-conscious and awkward in a social setting. Many display anxious or nervous behaviors, showing how tense they feel. Having direct eye contact makes them feel uneasy; instead, they will look in another direction, often making the person they are communicating with feel uncomfortable as well. At large gatherings, they may stand back and observe, and will usually engage in conversation with a person possessing a similar nature to their own. They have a knack for finding one another in a crowd and rarely partake in group discussions, unless it is about a topic they are well-versed in.

Thinkers avoid small talk at all costs. When forced to endure it, they will quickly zone out or redirect the conversation. Many find discussing personal issues and the details of people's lives rather annoying and uncomfortable; instead, they are more interested in discussing ideas and discoveries. They prefer to converse about things based on facts, ideas, histories or past illustrations.

They like to do lots of things; but rarely will they participate in anything until they feel competent. They prefer to read or research rather than watching sports. Their greatest vulnerability is to look stupid or made a fool of, and they will do anything to avoid either one.

Thinkers are prone to be somewhat distant. They feel emotions deeply; however, few provide many clues regarding their reaction to situations. They are very feeling-based like Supporters. A Supporter likes to share personal feelings in connecting with others, and Thinkers make decisions based on their sense of security. When they feel any insecurity, Thinkers rely on data gathering to feel confident they have enough evidence for evaluating the situation. Though they hide their emotions for safety and protection, Thinkers are not void of deep feelings.

Most are loners that like to have peace and quiet and do not do well in a crowded or noisy area. They need to have space where they can have much-needed time alone to process and contemplate. As a matter of fact, if they have spent time in a crowd, they will need extra quiet, alone time to regenerate and rejuvenate. Out of all four personality styles, the Thinkers enjoy their own company the most.

Thinkers are very curious and spend much of their time working to discern unifying themes and metaphysical truths that explain the underlying nature of things and how they work. They research and devour stacks of books on a topic and accurately assess all the constituent parts. It is important for them to understand the whole picture. Topics that interest them may be technology, philosophy, math, mechanics, engineering, psychology, religion or any science-based subject. Many people feel challenged and intellectually inadequate in a Thinker's presence.

They are motivated to understand the world around them and desire to explain, forecast and apply control over reality. Thinkers are natural scientists, people who explore and define the limitations of natural law. They want to know how things work in detail, the reason behind everything, and will work endlessly to reach solid conclusions.

Thinkers like solving problems by asking questions, by researching and coming up with new ideas and by using models. They need clear objectives and enough time to gather data and information, as well as time to analyze it before making a decision. Because their thinking is objective, they won't be satisfied with simple explanations but need to understand the principle or theory behind concepts. They need autonomy and like to work on projects independently.

Thinkers do not like having to make quick, uninformed decisions or being given unclear goals. They are quick to point out repetition or redundancy, having little patience for either.

Thinkers are serious and purposeful, the profound and brilliant minds of the world. They relate well to others through information and can have a reputation of boring people with too many details. Their challenge is to cultivate their social skills, learn how to show more emotion when they communicate and to acquire the skills of reading body language to gauge interest in what they are sharing.

They also have a quirky sense of humor and often use sarcastic remarks directed at a particular person in their banter. Their dry wit and sarcasm are frequently misunderstood by recipients, often causing them to react and bite back. Thinkers only strike when attacked or angry, and when they do, they use devastating blows that are intended to shut the other party up. It's their defense – but thankfully it is rarely used, only when they are out of self-esteem.

It is not uncommon for a Thinker to take the opposite viewpoint during a conversation to keep things interesting. They enjoy a healthy debate and delight in arguing their point of view. Some see this as antagonistic, but they see it as entertainment.

Thinkers serve others with their vast knowledge, vision, and innovation to improve performance and make significant changes in the world. They seek to improve systems in areas such as education, technology, politics, government or moving a company or project forward. They have minds that never quit and dream up new things and ideas that others have not thought of yet. Their ability to conceptualize before creating something gives them a clear edge. Though motivated by the pure acquisition of knowledge; control of their education is equally important to them, because they deem knowledge as power.

Thinkers derive much of their self-esteem from work. They are extremely focused and take their jobs very seriously. As mentioned earlier, most consider their work as play. Suitable careers for the Thinker personality are those that require intellect, vision, and independent thinking. Being gifted at conceptualizing, theorizing, and coordinating complex issues, they gravitate towards areas that need logical investigation. Many consider careers in law, accounting, medicine, science, technology, engineering, assisting a physician or maybe in mechanics. Most college or university professors are of this quadrant of people because once they learn something, they feel compelled to share their knowledge. Whatever career choice they make, they strive to be the best at it, often rising to the top in their profession and/or organization.

Thinkers are resourceful and always manage to get into careers that pay well. They plan ahead for their financial future and will only make a purchase when it's necessary. They will always research before making a purchase to ensure they get the best quality and value.

Competence and clarity of thought are a Thinker's chief assets. They comprise a small percentage of the population of bright people who are independent, creative, solution-oriented, cool-headed, and most often non-conforming. They are the Einsteins of the world. Thinkers are the ones who chart new territory and make discoveries that often have global impact.

A THINKER'S GIFTS AND TALENTS

All of us are here to use our gifts to make a contribution to the world. A dominant Thinker's gifts are a natural part of their DNA, making them effortless to use. Most of their gifts involve using their knowledge and competence to analyze, solve problems or invent something better, which is their primary purpose in life.

They are conceptual and represent ingenuity, persistence, and change. When Thinkers are allowed to express their unique gifts, it contributes to their overall success and happiness.

- Abstract thinking
- Competence
- Debating and questioning
- Philosophical ideas
- Visionary
- Persistent and determined
- Systematic insights
- Innovation
- Developing systems and models
- Evaluating and investigating
- Precise spelling and grammar
- Improving upon status quo
- Technical know-how
- Unemotional advice
- Intellectual triumphs
- Knowledge
- Logic
- Strategic processing

- Analyzing
- Making decisions based on facts
- Objectivity
- Insightfulness
- Perfectionism
- Conceptualizing
- Precise, concise, accurate work
- Generating ideas
- Independent processing
- Problem solving, fixing things
- Innovation
- Researching and exploring
- Self-control - cool, calm, collected
- Inventing
- Theoretical ideas
- Diagnosing
- Witty, dry humor

JOYS

Thinkers gain satisfaction, fulfillment, and joy from the following:

- Being acknowledged by professional colleagues
- Exploring new ideas

- High achievement and superior accomplishments
- Meeting challenges

- Solving problems
- Discovering new possibilities
- Demonstrating technical expertise
- Being recognized for original systems and new ideas
- Doing what can't be done
- Understanding and explaining complexities
- Creative freedom
- Humor and irony
- Time to think and analyze
- Research and reading to gain knowledge

VALUES

Values are an inner guide that directs a Thinker's actions and gives their life purpose and meaning.

CORE VALUE: Competence

- Accuracy
- Knowledge, wisdom, and expertise
- Intellectual achievement
- Logic
- Creativity and ingenuity
- Independence
- Analysis
- Ideas
- Precision
- Technology
- Self-control
- Self-sufficiency
- Innovation
- Truth and facts, data, information, and statistics
- Systematic approach and strategy
- Improvement

NEEDS

Meeting a Thinker's needs is a sure way to gain their cooperation. Their comfort, health, happiness, and success, depends on satisfying these needs through continued opportunities and experiences. When their needs are not satisfied, frustration and stress increase, which often leads to conflict; or worse, emotional or physical health problems.

- Privacy – peace and quiet

- To find solutions and make improvements
- Challenge – do what others say can't be done
- Autonomy - time to think, read, analyze
- Intellectual stimulation
- Facts, truth, and accuracy
- Information, data, and statistics
- To explore new ideas
- Research; being well-informed
- Flexibility
- Correct speech and grammar
- To be curious, inquiring, questioning, and skeptical
- To be objective
- To gain knowledge and wisdom; continually improving and learning
- Innovation – improving the status quo and creating change
- To make comparisons; look at pros and cons
- Competence, logic and sound reasoning
- Systems and technology that work well
- To be emotionally composed – not swayed by emotions or feelings
- To develop, diagnose, design, and invent

STRESSORS

A Thinker's capacity to succeed in life is significantly diminished when they experience the following:

- Senseless or unreasonable rules
- Emotional displays without logic
- Chaos and confusion
- Rigidity
- Lack of independence or freedom
- Appearing stupid
- Being unprepared or having to make quick decisions
- Incompetence in self or others
- Routine, redundancy and repetition

- Unclear goals and objectives
- Unfairness
- Equipment or technology failure
- Bad grammar
- Inability to display or use knowledge
- Loud noises and distractions
- Social functions and small talk
- Not knowing, understanding or having answers
- Mistakes
- Lack of options or time to properly analyze, study or gather data
- Judgments made based on beliefs or feelings, rather than verifiable evidence of facts
- Individuals who don't value wisdom, knowledge, and learning

REACTION TO STRESS

When Thinkers are stressed out or overwhelmed their personalities grow dim, and their positive characteristics do an about face. In this state, they often behave indecisively and will withdraw and stop communicating. They usually refuse to comply and get highly critical towards self and others. Many obsess and worry. To rebuild their self-esteem, they need time alone and someone to encourage them by pointing out their value, intelligence, and contribution.

When experiencing low self-esteem or stress, they may behave in the following ways:

- Insensitivity to feelings of others
- Contrary questioning
- Playing victim
- Becoming impatient
- Disapproval towards self and others
- Using words as a weapon to cut others down
- Withdrawing and distancing themselves
- Stubbornly refusing to comply or cooperate
- Analysis paralysis
- Feeling like no one gets them or understands them

- Breaking rules
- Having angry outbursts
- Blaming others, circumstances or technology
- Arrogant and argumentative attitude
- Depressed state

CHALLENGING AREAS FOR THE THINKER PERSONALITY STYLE

Every personality type has areas that challenge them. What challenges the Thinker personality style is social settings with pressure to small talk with people who they share little in common. They feel awkward in these settings and crave alone time where they can be with their thoughts and ideas.

With consistent practice, the challenging areas for the Thinker personality style become easier to deploy.

AREA OF CHALLENGE	NEED TO PRACTICE
Socializing, small talk, people skills, and social graces.	Learning the personality style differences so they can better their social and business interactions.
Having eye contact when talking with people.	Learning social etiquette and having eye contact.
Allowing conversation to flow. Responding quickly without analyzing and searching for purpose and meaning in the conversation.	Letting people know when they require time to think. Practice responding more rapidly without analyzing everything first.
Perfectionism.	Accepting that errors can happen.

AREA OF CHALLENGE	NEED TO PRACTICE
Labeling people as "stupid."	Accepting the personality style differences and recognizing that everyone is gifted. Intellect is only one of the many gifts people have.
Being less critical.	Holding their tongue instead of criticizing others, accepting that others can be a contribution. Learn to use softeners when communicating.
Pessimistic about new ideas.	Being open-minded and optimistic towards new ideas and new possibilities.
Being "right" all the time.	Being okay when they, or others, are "wrong."
Overanalyzing.	Trusting so quicker decisions or progress can be made.
Reading body language. Dumping data and talking when people have no interest in what they are saying.	Having eye contact and learning Body language so they can see cues and stop talking when others are not interested. Determining personality of the listener and using appropriate strategy for relaying information.
Taking chances for fear of looking stupid.	Taking chances and being okay with the outcome.

AREA OF CHALLENGE	NEED TO PRACTICE
Listening, without fixing.	Asking people if they are seeking a solution or a listening ear. Not every problem needs their fixing.
Following rules.	Instead of questioning the validity of rules, accepting that they are there for a reason.
Giving the "silent treatment."	Communicating and expressing rather than going silent which solves nothing.
Humor at the expense of others.	Being more sensitive and accepting that their humor is rare and not appreciated by most.
Fitting in, instead of feeling like an outsider.	Engaging with others, learning the four personality styles to mirror the behavior of others.
People that don't share their intellect.	Valuing and accepting the gifts others have.
Correcting people's grammar and speech.	Only doing so when someone solicits their help.
Procrastinating.	Trusting that they have enough data or information to get the job done or make the decision at hand. Just do it!

AREA OF CHALLENGE	NEED TO PRACTICE
Blaming circumstances, people or technology.	Being accountable.

TURN TO THINKERS FOR

Thinkers like to share their knowledge. Their logical approach allows them to troubleshoot and fix areas that require change or expertise.

ANALYTICAL SKILL – Thinkers are known to make sensible decisions by gathering required data and information. While pouring over information, they have the ability to visualize, articulate, conceptualize or solve the most complex of problems.

PERFECTION – They are very efficient and always look for ways to improve something. They are only happy when they have perfected their work.

FIXING THINGS – Thinkers are gifted at diagnosing problems and figuring out how to repair or fix things.

LOGICAL REASONING – Thinkers form sound judgments and conclusions by assessing a situation using logic, knowledge and proven methods of reasoning.

DEVELOPING SYSTEMS – Using a logical process, they plan, design, test and deploy new systems. Most software, engineering, or information systems were created by Thinkers. They are very methodical and will develop one step at a time.

PERSISTENCE – A Thinker does not give up easily. They will persevere, evaluating every aspect of how something works to come up with a viable result. Like Thomas Edison, if they don't get it right the first time, they persist until they get it right; always thinking, studying and learning better ways of doing things.

INVENTING – Thomas Edison stands as the greatest inventor of all time, and he was a Thinker. He would define a need and work on finding the solution. Thinkers follow the same pattern, using their analytical skills to identify a need, or problem, and work until a viable, practical answer is found and tested for efficiency. The greatest technological advances we enjoy today were likely the invention of a Thinker.

RESEARCHING – A Thinker can spend countless hours researching topics of interest with no concept of the time that has passed. They are thorough researchers who know where to find useful information. They always have a plethora of interesting topics they want to research and could easily spend an entire day doing so.

TECHNICAL KNOW HOW – Because their brains work in an analytical, systematic way, they can conceptualize how technical things work by connecting the dots. If you have a technical problem, they most often can fix it.

COMPETENCE – Because Thinkers have no margin for error, they educate themselves by gathering and studying information and data until they are confident that they come across as an expert, or at least as competent. They ensure that the fields they work in, or the discussions they have regarding an issue originate from a place of knowledge and education. When they do something, they do it well.

INTELLIGENCE – Thinkers are intellects. In conversations, they desire to dive into topics where they can share their knowledge and wisdom. In school, they were the nerdy academic achievers. They like information and data and never stop educating themselves on topics of interest. Their grammatical skills are far superior to the other personality styles.

VISION – Thinkers are always looking for ways to change the status quo.

They are known for bringing about the world's most renowned advances, developments, and inventions by establishing new systems and protocols. They are big picture, global thinkers and therefore concern themselves with the progress that will influence society. They are the Einsteins and Edisons of the world.

CONCEPTUALIZING – Their gifted logical minds link all the necessary steps (A-Z) together. Using a systematic approach, they examine the various scenarios, being mindful of the cause and effect, until they bring a concept to fruition.

INNOVATION – Gifted at coming up with new methods and ideas. They love taking on a challenge that others can't solve and will diligently work until they find an innovative solution.

INQUISITIVE – Thinkers inquire, research and ask questions. They are naturally curious and are eager for knowledge that will help them resolve a problem or contentious matter or will assist them in charting new ground. They love to study and ask questions regarding how and why things function the way they do.

ACCURACY – Thinkers are sticklers for accuracy and have little tolerance for error. Their systematic, analytical processing helps them develop things with absolute precision. Their slow, methodical way of doing things pretty much eliminates any margin for error.

KNOWLEDGE - Their insatiable thirst for knowledge only gets heightened when they learn more about their chosen topic through research. They will gather data and information on their favored topics until they know everything about it. Once they have a thorough knowledge on a subject, they get excited and automatically want to share it with others.

SOLVING PROBLEMS - They will study the problem until they have a resolution, pouring over the research and data they have gathered to ensure their solution is achievable. The more complicated the problem, the more charged and committed they are to solving it.

HOW THINKERS ARE VIEWED BY SELF AND OTHERS

Thinkers view their behavior as cool, calm, appropriate, and controlled. Others may not see their behavior in the same positive light, which is upsetting for a Thinker and often is a contributing factor to their social awkwardness and withdrawal.

Usually, a judgmental perception about a person's personality characteristics comes from people who least understand them; whose personality style lineup scores are the lowest in their category. Creating harmonious relationships involve looking through different lenses to understand our personality differences. Holding positive perceptions of others, by realizing how gifted they are, contributes to everyone's success.

PERCEIVES SELF AS	OTHERS MAY PERCEIVE THEM AS
Confident with superior intellect. A standard setter. Competent and precise.	An intellectual snob. Thinks they are better and smarter than everyone. Geek.
Has a keen sense for understanding complex information. Has an expansive comprehension of most topics and likes to share their wealth of knowledge with others.	A know-it-all. Close minded and condescending. Assumes that others should know as much as they do. Undervalues the talents in others by offering unwanted advice or information – data dumps.
Rational, reasonable, logical, objective, focused on facts rather than the feelings and opinions of others. Task focused. Unemotional.	Insensitive, uncaring, arrogant, lacks emotion and mercy. Only cares about facts, not people. Cold hearted.

PERCEIVES SELF AS	OTHERS MAY PERCEIVE THEM AS
Visionary, creative, inventive, innovative with original ideas. Concerned about improving or changing the status quo. Competent. Believes in hard work and only welcomes praise for high standards of performance.	Demanding without recognizing the gifts others have. Insists that everything be done correctly and logically; the way they would do it. Gets annoyed when others don't comprehend or understand. Expects everyone to perform to their standards.
Independent and private, enjoys their own company. Will connect with others with similar interests when necessary. Sees no value in small talk.	Afraid to open up, anti-social, unfriendly, serious, unappreciative of others. Not a team player. Social outcast. Has no interest in people.
Precise with high expectations. Can spot inconsistencies and flaws and helps others improve by pointing them out.	Perfectionist. Unrealistic. Demands that others adhere to their high standards of performance. Degrading, harsh criticizers.
Self-controlled, unemotional, cool, calm and collected.	Cold – afraid to show emotion. Lacks feelings or social graces. Serious and unapproachable.
Has extensive vocabulary. Help others improve their grammar by pointing out any grammatical errors.	Acts superior - uses big words to show off. Embarrasses people by correcting their grammar. Cruel.
Knowledgeable with the ability to research and collect pertinent data on various topics of interest. Likes to educate others with their new-found knowledge.	A walking library of information. Show off and know-it-all. Data dumps and shares too many details about what they know. Does not pick up on cues that others are not interested.

PERCEIVES SELF AS	OTHERS MAY PERCEIVE THEM AS
Having the ability to reprimand and set people straight. Points out errors so, people will learn and avoid them in the future.	Focuses on what is wrong instead of what is right. Lacks mercy. Has to have the last word. Has no regard for the feelings of others. Self-righteous.
Good at analysis, able to find imperfections and deficiencies by researching the facts.	Critical fault finder. Looks for errors and mistakes with a condescending, judgmental attitude.
Witty and entertaining with a funny sense of humor.	Mean and demeaning, uses cynicism and sarcasm to make fun at the expense of others. Not funny!
Deep thinker – analytical. Takes the necessary time to think things through before making a decision or taking action.	Thinks too much. Gets analysis paralysis from overthinking everything. Slow to make decisions and reach conclusions.
Finds the truth by probing and asking "why" questions.	Probing and argumentative. Interrogates and focuses on the negative.

PART IV

Effective Communication with the Four Personality Styles

"Your ability to communicate is an important tool in
your pursuit of your goals, whether it is with your family,
your co-workers or your clients and customers."
Les Brown, Author, and Motivational Speaker

Chapter 9

Effective Communication with the Supporter Personality Style

HOW SUPPORTERS COMMUNICATE

Supporters are all about people, relationships, and fostering growth, both in themselves and others. When they communicate, they are polite and their attention is always focused on establishing or reestablishing the relationship first and foremost. They establish good eye contact and can talk and listen endlessly, nodding and responding when people are talking. You can always rely on them to give an honest answer to a question.

Below are a few words that describe a Supporter's communication style

Friendly – Relaxed, approachable and non-threatening with a gentle, polite or enthusiastic voice. They like to be acknowledged and make it a point to acknowledge others. Supporters readily greet others with a kind word, handshake, smile, hug, comment, question, or conversation.

Helpful – They are energized by helping others and will offer their assistance, feeling compelled to help others whenever a need or a worthwhile cause is presented.

Takes Time to Connect – Will usually stop what they are doing to acknowledge others and give them the attention they deserve. Supporters read people well and, like a chameleon they are able to adapt to the style of the person they converse with. They welcome conversations with anyone – it could be the store clerk, the homeless or a CEO. Supporters will take interest in and provide support for what's said.

Expresses Feelings and Emotions – They speak with feeling and emotion in their voice as they empathize with the dramas of life. Their body language and expressive words reveal their mood. Supporters wear their hearts on their sleeves.

Sees the Best in Everyone – Supporters are optimistic and always see the best in others or situations. They will give people the benefit of the doubt or another chance, even when others have given up hope. They have faith in people's good nature and are gifted at finding something good to say about everyone. They pay attention to body language to gauge how others are doing.

Fosters Peace and Harmony – Supporters want everyone to get along and be happy. They will do their best to sidestep conflict or negative talk to ensure there is harmony.

Empathetic – Supporters can enter another's world and feel and experience it with them, based on the individual's point of view. They avoid imposing their own beliefs and often adapt or make decisions based on the desires and needs of others.

Creative – Supporters are highly imaginative and sometimes embellish points when communicating examples or stories. They generally welcome a conversation with most anyone and love discussing ideas, insights, and concepts as they pertain to people, the human condition, and the future.

Indirect – Supporters will likely interpret people's bluntness, fast-moving speech or loudness as rude. When Supporters convey information or an experience, their explanations may seem lengthy and challenging to follow. They may soften painful truths, using phrases such as: "I don't want to be any trouble; but…" or "Is it okay if…," to spare hurting the feelings of others. Supporters also say, "Sorry" often and seem apologetic when they ask for something or make requests.

Reads Between the Lines – Supporters are attentive listeners. Instead of taking everything at face value, Supporters rely on instincts and their intuition to guide them, often looking behind actions and words for a deeper meaning and true intentions. They are quick to detect phoniness and lies, and are very good at discerning false motives and actions.

Personal – Supporters enjoy sharing stories about personal aspects of their life which makes it easy to get to know them. They routinely use "I" statements; often sharing intimate details about their life, if they think it may deepen a relationship. To validate and include others, they will comment on or elaborate on what others say. They express acceptance, appreciation, and affection for others genuinely and effortlessly.

Polite and Compassionate – Supporters are polite and will rarely interrupt without first checking if it's okay when someone is speaking. A Supporter's focus is always on relationships, harmony, and comfort. They nod and respond when people are talking. They are quick to apologize if they notice that the other person is feeling disregarded or uncomfortable in a conversation. However, they will dig in their heels, put up walls and become very stubborn if their values have been violated. Threatening language would only be used if they felt betrayed or endangered.

HOW SUPPORTERS LISTEN

Supporters listen to what the speaker needs and how they can help. They focus on more than just words in a conversation; they listen for the meaning behind the message. They evaluate what they see, hear, and feel about the speaker and the message being communicated. They listen deeply and assess the speaker's values to see if they are in alignment with their own. Supporters will give the speaker the benefit of the doubt, if they feel the person is sincere and has a caring attitude towards others.

When they have discerned that it's okay to relate to the speaker, they will decide how they feel about the message. No message will be fully understood and accepted if the relationship is not first established.

TIPS FOR COMMUNICATING WITH THE SUPPORTER STYLE

DO

- Start by connecting - smile and be optimistic
- Maintain eye contact while talking to them
- Speak in a friendly, non-threatening tone of voice
- Listen attentively to what they say without interrupting them
- Ask personal questions and be prepared to share your feelings and thoughts
- Be considerate and let them express their feelings and emotions
- Include and involve them in the conversation
- Share what you appreciate about them – let them know they matter
- Use appropriate physical touch (pat on the back, handshake, hug, etc.)
- Acknowledge and accept their individuality and uniqueness
- Be honest and sincere
- Be patient as they relay information, tell a story or process

DON'T

- Be rude or cut them off while they are speaking
- Shame or ridicule their creativity, imagination or dreams
- Be critical of their sensitivity, feelings and emotions
- Expect them to be confrontational
- Compare them to others
- Ignore or isolate them

- Take advantage of their good heart, kindness, caring, and generosity
- Lie to them
- Put others down by being cruel or talking badly about them
- Be controlling, aggressive or harsh with them
- Tease, embarrass or humiliate them or make them a subject of sarcasm

SUPPORTERS LIKE TO TALK ABOUT

- Personal relationship and human condition issues
- Ideas, insights, and concepts
- Feel-good stories
- Art and creative pursuits
- Their children or families
- Spiritual matters or self-development
- Healthy living
- Outdoor nature adventures

COMMUNICATION TIPS FOR SUPPORTERS

- Practice saying, "No" to favors and requests you don't have time, energy or desire to do, as your tendency is to overcommit
- Eliminate drama in conversations when you need others to take you more seriously
- Avoid taking on guilt or negative emotions of others – choose to be happy, honest and free of things that are emotionally draining
- Don't take everything personally; work to be objective and ask for clarification or the intentions behind what was said
- Say, "Yes" to things that resonate with you, not to what others expect of you
- Discern body language and conclude when people don't want to hear more about your subject
- Be open to constructive feedback without putting your defense up – it could be helpful

- Don't make people guess what you need; instead speak up and let your needs be known
- Stop apologizing for everything; especially saying, "I'm sorry" when it's not your fault
- Spend time with other Supporters who understand you, and want to participate in deep, personal communication or events that are meaningful to you

CHAPTER 10

Effective Communication with the Promoter Personality Style

HOW PROMOTERS COMMUNICATE

Promoters love interacting and have a substantial network of people to draw from. They need freedom when conversing with others. Introverted Promoters display less intensity than that of extroverted Promoters. They are friendly people and read others well, sometimes mirroring in conversations, to build quick rapport.

Below are a few words that describe a Promoter's communication style

Confident – Promoters are enthusiastic and stimulating. They speak with certainty, sureness and decisiveness; whether they know what they are talking about or not.

Loud – Can be boisterous and intense and may turn the volume up to ensure people hear them. They love to express themselves and often exaggerate to make their story entertaining. They don't mind being the center-of-attention and will seek it.

"Now" Oriented – They talk more than they listen and may interrupt when they want to respond, or will complete other's sentences, instead of waiting for them to finish.

Casual – Promoters are informal and may use slang, profanity or popular phrases when they communicate. They prefer to be on a first name basis with individuals. They are friendly, playful and charming; putting everyone at ease as they build rapport.

Desire to Speak in the Moment – Promoters process out loud and speak as soon as they have a thought, opinion or comment. They tend to make quick promises that are forgotten almost as fast as they are made.

Quick – They are action-oriented and hate to wait for answers to questions. They will often change subjects before their listener is ready. They appreciate people that are decisive and give immediate feedback. They also provide swift feedback to others.

Brief – Promoters are very direct and spend little time with "How are you?" or other greetings. They like to get to the point quickly without wasting their time or breath. Promoters make sure every moment counts.

Straightforward – They state things with clarity and detail, leaving no room for confusion or doubt. They don't try to soften delivery, telling it "as it is" in a bold, straightforward, uncensored fashion.

In Motion – Promoters crave mobility. They often multi-task, check phone messages, fidget, move around, or work while you are talking to them. Most Promoters have the ability to be productive during a conversation.

Flexible – They may initially agree with you; but then may change their mind, should a better option be presented. Promoters reserve the right to change their mind, often doing so midstream.

Varied – Unless Promoters are directly involved in the topic being discussed, their attention span is minimal. They seek opportunities and like to have options and choices. They are capable of switching gears at a moment's notice, changing from one topic to another without hesitation. They will tune you out if there is too much information or data being shared.

Involved – Promoters like to laugh, play, tell jokes and relay stories in a larger than life fashion. They are quick-witted and find humor in the mundane. They are very charismatic. Extroverted Promoters are known to use large gestures, body movements, and animated facial and voice expressions when relaying their message. They delight in spontaneity and action, often arguing just for fun.

HOW PROMOTERS LISTEN

Promoters listen for usefulness, relevance, impact, and entertainment. They lose interest quickly if the conversation is not stimulating, is detailed or lengthy, and if it does not immediately reveal useful information. They prefer to receive information in bullet point format.

When a person speaks, Promoters listen for their motives; what they want, need or expect. They listen in the present, to figure out what action they can take, with what is being said. They may share a quick joke, seize a challenge, or set out to accomplish something that requires courage, skill or strength.

TIPS FOR COMMUNICATING WITH THE PROMOTER STYLE

DO

- Be friendly, energetic, upbeat and excited in their presence
- Let them process audibly to share their excitement or blow off steam
- Keep up with their speed when you talk to them
- Be direct and look at them when you're talking

- Give them only small amounts of information, to keep their attention
- Lighten up and allow for fun, playful interactions with them
- Talk about the big picture and possibilities, using lots of examples
- Provide some structure for them; yet be flexible and allow them to change their mind
- Show appreciation for their stories, jokes and playful nature
- Respect their need to stay busy doing things while conversing

DON'T

- Be rigid or authoritative with them or tell them what to do
- Ignore them or interrupt them when they are telling a story or joke
- Be intimidated by their energy
- Be surprised at their variable nature or be offended when they change their minds
- Spend too much time talking about serious or sad subjects
- Force them to be too serious about life
- Demand that they stick to a strict schedule
- Look in a different direction if you want them to listen to you
- Write them off as unreliable because of their happy-go-lucky nature
- Tell them their ideas are stupid or unachievable
- Make them sit and listen for extended periods of time, without movement

PROMOTERS LIKE TO TALK ABOUT

- Stories, testimonials or jokes
- Fun adventures
- Sports, physical activities or challenges
- Hobbies
- Clever approaches and ways of dealing with something
- Winning strategies
- What's possible; ideas and benefits
- The latest news

COMMUNICATION TIPS FOR PROMOTERS

- Be aware of how blunt you may sound and modify your speech to fit the listener's personality style
- Be patient; listen and wait for a response before proceeding – give people time to think and process
- Use your insight into people, to perceive what they need from you – this may mean that you'll pause and stop what you are doing, make eye contact, and do what is required to connect with others, on their level
- Save your colorful stories and jokes for those who will appreciate them
- Don't interrupt; let others complete their thoughts before you jump in to share yours
- Think before you make commitments – get in the habit of giving yourself twenty-four hours to think things through
- Acknowledge others instead of seeking all the attention – learn to praise people in ways that are meaningful to them
- Instead of barking out orders; learn to say, "please" and, "thank you" when giving directions or making requests
- Be your word – if you make a commitment or promise, stick to it
- Spend time with other Promoters who understand you and won't take offense at your direct, playful communication style

Chapter 11

Effective Communication with the Planner Personality Style

HOW PLANNERS COMMUNICATE

A Planner's primary role is to be responsible. They tend to come across in a business-like manner. They discuss structure, responsibility and rules of life, such as "should" and "should nots." They often point out what's "right" or "wrong." They are clear, direct and to the point in their communication. Generally, they are approachable and friendly; but always cautious and often rushed. They have firm views and only share personal information when they know someone well.

Planners will give eye contact for short moments; but are uncomfortable with doing this for long periods of time. They may look in your general direction; but over your head. Their speech is fast-paced, decisive and quick.

Below are a few words that describe a Planner's communication style

In Writing – They are perfectionists and demand accuracy. They like things recorded, so the details are there for future reference and they don't have to rely on their memory. They prefer things in writing, so they have precise documentation with facts and details, in case questions arise regarding the conversation, timeline or responsibility.

Purposeful – Planners like to plan every detail of their day and prefer to adhere to their timelines, especially at work. They get aggravated when people interrupt their schedule and get frustrated if they are wasting time chit-chatting instead of being productive doing something. To ensure they stay on course, they state the reason for their conversation up front and bring it to a close once they have discussed its purpose.

Appropriate – Planners are cautious and conservative. They stay on topic, like to be politically correct and will use proper language, avoiding slang or incorrect wording. Planners are very respectful and rarely fool around or tell jokes; especially in a business setting, where they deem this behavior inappropriate. They will correct those, who are not following the proper norms for the situation. They may be able to relax their serious side in social situations, where that kind of thing is accepted.

Task Focused – Once they have established the purpose of a conversation, Planners most likely will center their discussion on accomplishing the goal; they like to stay on topic. Generally, they lack interest in what's said, unless it is about the matter at hand. They get frustrated when people disrupt the conversation by interjecting comments or attempting to change the subject. They give their undivided attention to the interaction and expect the same in return.

Loyal – Planners show loyalty and respect to their family, the organization they work or volunteer for, and their community. The only time they would criticize anyone is if they have been disloyal or broken too many rules. They are dedicated citizens that uphold policies, rules, and customs.

Predictable – Planners are consistently reliable and will speak and respond predictably. Rarely will they surprise anyone with a last-minute request, unless they are experiencing a tremendous amount of stress.

Traditional – Planners place a high value on tradition and proudly follow customs that have been passed on to them through generations. When they communicate, they often reference the way things were done in the past and prefer to stick with what they know and can rely on.

Chronological – They relate information or events in chronological order, explaining the entire linear process. If they are interrupted when relaying information, they will start from the beginning and describe the whole sequence, to ensure they include everything. Planners don't like to start in the middle. When a conversation is begun, they like to establish the purpose of it up front. They will often ask for history or background, to get their bearings on the situation or project. Planners listen for details, responsibility, purpose, and understanding.

Detail Oriented – Planners are very specific; sharing details and logistics, rather than generalities or interpretations. They always provide clearly defined instructions.

Closure – Planners desire to finish one thought or topic at a time. When conversing with a Planner, they will let you know when they are bringing the conversation to a close. They don't want anyone to be left guessing what's expected. Planners are uncomfortable with too many options left open and may insist that a choice is made. Once a selection has been made, they will focus on fulfilling the requirements to satisfy the decision.

Tried and True – Planners like things that have a proven track record. They are hesitant to embrace a new way and they prefer things that are tried and true. They look at the past for references on how things should be done and will defend the successful approaches. Planners are slow to embrace change.

Judgments – Planners judge what another individual says, by whether the person is saying or doing what is right or wrong. They give their views in an authoritarian way, using words like "should" and "should not" followed by their reasoning. Once a Planner feels confident and clear on what the correct action should be in a situation, they find facts to back up their thinking. Once they institute a standard and back it up with evidence, or decide upon a particular value, their communication leaves no room for a varied interpretation. They ensure their listener knows what they are talking about and what action is expected as a result of their conversation.

Accountable – Planners like to know what is expected of them so they can conform and follow the rules without disappointing anyone. They will ask questions until they reach clarity. Once clear, they commit to the request or task at hand and can be relied upon to bring it to completion.

HOW PLANNERS LISTEN

Planners listen for details and responsibility. They gather information, so they understand their role. Planners are always concerned with whether something is right or wrong and they will listen for the speaker's intentions. They are more comfortable in a conversation when they have determined the appropriateness of the interaction or response and will ask themselves, "What is my duty?" or "What should I do with this information?"

TIPS FOR COMMUNICATING WITH THE PLANNER STYLE

DO

- Follow through with what you said you'd do
- Be punctual
- Acknowledge them when they do something well
- Give them time to plan things
- Keep your agreements with them
- Let them know what you wish to discuss ahead of time and know details of what you want to relay in your conversations
- Complete one topic before moving on to the next
- Be specific when making a request, to ensure they understand what is required
- Recognize their need for equal give and take – if they invite you for dinner, reciprocate
- Give them adequate time to present their topic of discussion
- Take responsibility for your actions by apologizing when necessary

DON'T

- Surprise them or expect them to be spontaneous
- Be wasteful or extravagant or ask them to spend their money frivolously
- Use vulgar or profane language around them
- Expect them to challenge the law or established rules
- Insist they make decisions without all the facts
- Force them to take risks or ask them to think on their feet without adequate preparation time
- Interrupt them, until they have completed their sentence or thought
- Small talk - get to the point of the conversation
- Rush them or ask them to speed up
- Expect them to take a risk or step out of their comfort zone
- Say you will do something and not follow through
- Demand too much immediate change

PLANNERS LIKE TO TALK ABOUT

- What has worked in the past
- Responsibility and structure
- How things "should" or "should not" be in life
- What the bottom line is or the next step
- Family history and traditions
- Positions to help with or projects needing to be worked on
- Cost and time-sharing tips and strategies
- Streamlining or organizational techniques

COMMUNICATION TIPS FOR PLANNERS

- Be patient with people who don't operate in the disciplined, agenda-driven fashion you do
- Be open-minded and accept that there are different ways to achieve the desired outcome in a conversation – it doesn't always have to unfold chronologically

- Practice pausing in conversation to see the big picture; instead of honing in on the details
- Instead of judging whether a person's actions are "right" or "wrong" on the onset of a conversation, consider letting them finish speaking before you form an opinion
- Don't stifle creativity in those who like to brainstorm and think out loud
- Practice allowing people to be self-expressed in their verbal communication and actions
- Accept that others have different skills and values than you, without wanting to change them
- Be aware of how blunt and controlling you may sometimes sound and modify your speech
- Practice sharing personal information, to connect with those who relate that way
- Spend time with other Planners who understand you; who won't take offense at your need to plan everything, including time for fun

Chapter 12

Effective Communication with the Thinker Personality Style

HOW THINKERS COMMUNICATE

Thinkers generally communicate to gain or share information and seldom focus on establishing or strengthening relationships in a conversation. They like to share ideas and concepts with people who understand their communication style. When conversing, they focus on the subject at hand and relay their thoughts in a logical and precise way, taking time to think on what is asked of them, before they respond.

Thinkers may speak with a monotone voice and show few verbal cues as to their emotions. They are uncomfortable with steady eye contact and will look in a different direction when they speak to someone, often missing out on non-verbal messages revealed by a person's tonality, body language and facial expressions.

Below are a few words that describe a Thinker's communication style

Purposeful – Thinkers view small talk as a waste of time and brain cells and therefore avoid it at all cost. They prefer to get to the point, so they can discuss the pertinent information. A classic line for many Thinkers is, "And your point is?" They prefer to discuss one topic at a time.

Private – Thinkers generally do not talk about relationships or personal matters. Instead, they prefer to talk about ideas, information, and strategies.

Logical – They may seem cold to those who don't understand the Thinker style of communicating. They have deep feelings; but they don't display them freely. They are objective and use analysis and reasoning to reach conclusions. Thinkers are logical and concise.

Think Before They Respond – Thinkers are generally people of few words, especially the introverted Thinkers. They like to ponder the subject at hand and how to answer correctly. Many don't feel the need to do a lot of talking. They only participate when they know about the topic discussed.

Irritated with Laziness – Thinkers get irritated when people ask them for a solution, before they stop to think or make an attempt to figure something out for themselves first.

Avoids Redundancy – Thinkers will get annoyed and mentally leave a conversation if a person overexplains something, especially if they have more knowledge on the topic than the person doing the explaining.

Theoretical – Thinkers are always exploring ways to improve things and like to speak of new ideas and future plans. They avoid the "tried and "true" methods and seek after fresh ideas, focusing on what's possible. They are hypothetical and abstract. They use hand movements or models to explain ideas and concepts.

Like the Big Picture – They envision an idea or concept first, before honing in on the details of the big picture; and they like others to follow suit.

Explores Ideas – Thinkers love exchanging thoughts and having discussions about topics of interest with people that understand what they are talking about. Before they invest time listening to others, they want to establish the credibility of the speaker. They like to embellish concepts.

Asks Questions – Thinkers often bypass emotional bonding, as they only want the facts or data. They question most things to ensure they fully understand and like to debate while calculating the pros and cons. They may express a controversial opinion to test the strength of the opposing argument. They respond negatively to inaccurate information or incompetence. They are quick to point out mistakes and like to play "devil's advocate."

Use Big Words – Thinkers articulate well using high-level vocabulary, analogies, and metaphors; they are very precise in their conversations. They are also known to correct those who use incorrect grammar when they have dialogue.

Communicates with Conviction – Thinkers use strong statements and can be very persuasive and convincing when they communicate a point. In a conversation, they look for compliance, belief, or agreement in the listener.

Wry Sense of Humor – They see the humor in situations. Thinkers are witty, observant, and frequently use sarcasm and creative word puns which are not always welcomed by others.

HOW THINKERS LISTEN

Thinkers listen for detailed information, wanting to know the purpose of the communication. They are accustomed to having people approach them to solve problems or exchange material. Thinkers tune out anyone with extreme emotions, as well as subjects that hold little interest for them. They listen for the issues or challenges that need to be solved and will jump to solution mode, with no outward signs of compassion or empathy.

TIPS FOR COMMUNICATING WITH THE THINKER STYLE

DO

- Give them logical, factual explanations

- Allow them time to think before you pressure them for an answer
- Expect them to take a leadership role in conversations that are about topics they are well versed in
- Earn their respect by backing up statements with facts and truths
- Acknowledge their intelligence and innovative ideas
- Be prepared to present data to support your ideas
- Recognize their need to get to the point quickly
- Debate with them for fun and defend your position
- Provide a context, outcome, or purpose for the discussion and stick to the subject at hand
- Use proper grammar; know the meaning of the big words you use
- Allow them time to explain the purpose of their vision or work

DON'T

- Small talk with them
- Ask personal questions or expect them to share their feelings or emotions
- Get offended with their "why?" or "what do you mean?" questions, as they seek more specific factual information
- Over-explain things, because they probably know more about the topic than you do
- Try to force them to be social
- Embarrass them, especially in front of others
- Let your emotions erupt when conversing or arguing with them
- Be indecisive
- Misunderstand their humor and take everything they say personally
- Be insulted if they don't show interest in what you share; they only like giving an ear to discussions they see as valuable, logical or intriguing
- Interrupt them, allow them to complete what they are saying
- Finish their sentences for them
- Tell them their ideas are stupid or attack their intellect

THINKERS LIKE TO TALK ABOUT

- Concepts, ideas, and possibilities
- Future plans
- Solutions to problems
- The latest proven discovery
- Their most recent findings on a particular topic
- Statistics and figures
- Improvements and how to change the status quo
- Topics of interest may be science, mechanics, engineering, politics, etc.

COMMUNICATION TIPS FOR THINKERS

- Use softeners when questioning others, to ensure they don't feel interrogated
- Save the debate; not everyone appreciates playing mental chess
- Learn to listen without fixing - ask if they are seeking a solution or want a listening ear
- Build rapport, before you charge ahead with your agenda
- Allow others to express their feelings and emotions, as that is how they may need to process
- Figure out what your significant relationships need and appreciate to feel close to you; and accommodate them, even if it doesn't seem practical or logical
- Share something positive about a person before you point out any flaws, inconsistencies or discrepancies, so they don't feel criticized
- Request time to think and ponder what is being said; instead of going silent, where the listener feels ignored
- Avoid data dumping when asked to describe something – know what each personality style requires - some only want bullet point explanations, while others want the details
- Practice taking an interest in people's personal lives by asking questions about them

PART V

The Four Personality Styles at Work

"The two things in life you are in total
control over are; you're attitude and your effort."
Billy Cox

Chapter 13

Appreciating the Supporter at Work

Supporters work best in an open environment, where they can interact with others. Being isolated will not bring out their best attributes, nor will they perform well at work. Because they need relationships and friendships, they appreciate an "open door" policy, as it helps build a cohesive team.

Their workspace is warm and personal, and their number one concern is that people are happy. Family photos, posters with motivational sayings, flowers and things their children made are displayed to create an inviting, home-like atmosphere. They dress for comfort in natural fabrics, that are soft and often colorful, to personalize their artistic side. Supporters have an enthusiastic, friendly, supportive and genuine approach, always extending a welcome to anyone entering their doors.

On the job, they need to have peace and calm. It is important for Supporters to work in a harmonious environment where they can have a positive interaction with their co-workers on a regular basis. Supporters feel empowered when they are allowed to provide help, support, and encouragement to others. They do not thrive in a work environment filled with tension, arguing, or feuding.

They perform best in a non-competitive setting and get energized by positive feedback for a job well-done. Supporters need feedback on an on-going basis and like recognition for their accomplishments. Because they thrive on human interaction, lack of involvement with others drains their energy and will keep them from being peak performers.

Supporters love team building and team collaboration, working together to make goals a reality. They are great at supporting and motivating team members and will cheer everyone on to success. They like to be included and asked for input; and, have a creative way of problem solving and looking at things. Dealing with people issues or being solicited to do something that requires artistic creativity is their strong suit. Planning a company event would bring them great satisfaction.

It's important to point out what the purpose of a task is to a Supporter, because they like for everything they do to have meaning. Supporters are great at mentoring, teaching and training. These roles satisfy their need to help others succeed.

Supporters need open, honest communication and are willing to listen to people who are struggling with personal or work issues. Their intuition will guide them to give the troubled person empathy and acceptance. They make excellent mediators in the workplace. Supporters will help whenever a need arises; no task is too small for them.

Supporters are good at making friends wherever they go and like spending their coffee breaks or lunch breaks building meaningful relationships. They are loyal and sensitive to the needs of others; providing a listening ear to anyone who needs it. If anyone is new or standing alone, they will be the first to befriend them.

Supporters need to feel useful and love being asked to participate in support roles. They make the best team players, because of their willingness to follow and strengthen their leaders. Supporters help their teams grow as they accomplish their mission and goals together.

ON THE JOB, SUPPORTERS EXCEL AT

- Using their natural gifts of communication, nurturing and supporting
- Creative ideas and innovation
- Building relationships that hold their team together

- Giving service to others and helping with tasks, that no one else wants to do
- Personnel teaching, training and mentoring
- Creating a harmonious, peaceful work atmosphere and cheering up those who need it
- Being optimistic and cooperative
- Social or relationship related tasks
- Inspiring and motivating everyone to be successful
- Showing appreciation and caring support to the team

WORK FRUSTRATIONS AND STRESSORS FOR SUPPORTERS

- When performance is priority over people
- Unresolved conflict and disharmony
- Having a role that separates them from other people
- Unclear expectations and tight deadlines
- No positive feedback for work performed
- Being excluded or ignored by others
- Repetitive, mundane tasks that don't require interaction
- Not being able to have input or share their ideas
- Boring routines and rigid rules with no flexibility
- No social interaction, no touching or personal sharing
- No chance to use their imagination or skills - no creative outlet
- Negative people, gossiping, name calling or criticism
- No collaboration on projects
- Deadlines, paperwork, and too many details
- Censorship, being micro-managed or having to clock in/out
- Lack of team spirit
- No opportunity to mentor or teach others
- Lack of honesty and integrity
- Competition – because this means someone has to lose; and they want everyone to win

A SUPPORTER'S VALUE TO A TEAM

Supporters are gifted at building the relationships that unite a team and keep it cohesive. They are masters at interacting, motivating, and cheering the team on. They promote cooperation and collaboration. They make sure everyone feels like they belong and will be the first ones to welcome new team members.

A SUPPORTER'S IDEAL ROLE IN A PROJECT

They are not interested in leading or analyzing the project but they will give constant support to it. They provide encouragement to the team at every juncture, cheering everyone on towards personal growth and success. Supporters are peak performers when they are asked to use their creative imagination to problem solve, or are asked to help and support in any way, even with undesirable tasks that they understand need doing.

HOW TO IMPROVE THE JOB PERFORMANCE OF A SUPPORTER

- Create a warm and personal working atmosphere
- Recognize their full worth by showing that they are needed and appreciated
- Give them freedom and time to display their feelings and heal emotional wounds
- Have frequent open and honest interactions
- Let them contribute to workplace ambiance
- Create a harmonious working environment void of conflict and hostility
- Provide frequent one-on-one feedback
- Show your support, caring, and appreciation by touch, a hug, or a handshake
- Praise their creative approach and imagination at work
- Utilize their natural gift of communication, nurturing, and people-oriented ideas

Chapter 14

Appreciating the
Promoter at Work

Promoters are highly intelligent and creative. Their minds are drawn in many different directions, moving at a rapid pace. They are always generating new ideas, associations, possibilities and witty remarks. They think and process very quickly and therefore like to be where the action is.

Throw Promoters into a stressful crisis, and they will function better than any of the other personality styles. They remain calm and solution oriented, while others may fall apart. Promoters lead with their ability to act on a moment's notice, directing and delegating what has to happen to solve the issue. Promoters may even create a crisis when things seem uneventful, just to add some spice and excitement to life. They like to celebrate their victories and keep quiet about their so-called defeats, until they sort out what went wrong. Promoters claim there are no failures and view such events as an opportunity to learn and grow.

Promoters excel at competitive sports, advertising, performing arts, sales, marketing, negotiating or any hands-on occupation where they can interact with people. They are skilled with tools and gadgets and are willing to help others who struggle with them. Promoters can master anything they put their minds to achieving. They prefer information and direction in bullet-point format, keeping it as brief and simple as possible. Schedules, details, paperwork and budgets will stifle their creativity in seconds; and, following through on any of these is not their strong suit.

Promoters are self-motivated and like to be excellent at any job they take on, as they seek to master it. Gifted at streamlining procedures, by eliminating unnecessary steps, allows them to complete a task quicker than most. Multi-tasking is second nature for a Promoter; they can talk on the phone, text, and do a task all at the same time. They are most productive in informal environments.

They operate best when allowed to lead, motivate, and negotiate. Promoters always rise to any challenge and will surprise you with their innovation to win. Cornered by rules, regulations, policies, and procedures that have to be adhered to will silently kill a Promoter's spirit; after all, they break the rules and think policies and procedures are limiting.

When it comes to brainstorming, Promoters are masters. They intuitively know when an idea is brilliant, solid and sound, and immediately go to work on how to bring it to fruition. As long as they are excited about an idea and have freedom and flexibility; they will stay in action, accomplishing amazing things, earning a reputation of being a "Mover and Shaker." On a team, they work well with the Planners who can bring their ideas to completion and take care of any steps they don't like to do. When they have an assistant to whom they can delegate details, they are unstoppable, focusing on the "big picture," charting the course, creating and executing some impressive projects.

Promoters are outgoing, athletic, and humorous, which reflects in their workspace. Their office tends to look messy, with random articles or piles of paper everywhere. It is not uncommon to see tools and a sports bag or sports equipment somewhere in their office. They surround themselves with conversation starters and articles they deem as fun or attention grabbing, such as; joke items, funny sayings, action pictures, trophies, and rewards. Their office is exciting and fun to match their personalities. Their dress is colorful and trendy and they are always welcoming and talkative.

Promoters are energetic and have a difficult time sitting still, especially during long drawn out meetings. They prefer to be actively doing something rather than sitting and discussing it. They are stimulated by novelty and uncertainty; this gives them a chance to create something new. As long as they can take action, Promoters will pour their energy into completing the task.

They are not afraid of conflict or controversy and often use their excellent negotiation skills to resolve issues quickly. Gifted at influencing and convincing others, they make the best deals; and with their persistence, they most often get what they want.

Promoters have a warm, engaging demeanor; and are charismatic, persuasive and talkative. They are invigorated by social interaction and networking and have extensive connections, which makes them a great resource for service or business contacts. Their social prowess is what helps to develop and reinforce their self-esteem and self-image. They know how to work a crowd, engaging and charming their audiences with their passion and optimism. Promoters love attention, recognition and applause.

ON THE JOB, PROMOTERS EXCEL AT

- Confident leadership
- Enrolling others into their vision, inspiring them to take action
- Being a peak performer; competing and winning
- Generating and implementing ideas
- Crisis management, problem-solving and finding quick solutions
- Negotiating - gifted at gaining the cooperation of others and getting them on their side
- Making the work environment fun-filled, with entertaining ways of doing things
- Brainstorming and thinking outside the box
- Planning company events and making them a big success
- Spotting good opportunities and taking brisk action
- Direct communication; not wishy-washy, but clear and precise
- Change – they can switch course or pace quickly
- Multi-tasking and work that requires chance, risk or quick action

WORK FRUSTRATIONS FOR PROMOTERS

- Rigidness and lack of flexibility
- Slow people or slow progress
- Individuals who use their authority to force results
- Not being asked for ideas, input or involvement
- Inactivity
- Not being asked to solve problems in a crisis
- Adhering to policies and procedures, rules and regulations
- Lack of communication and social interaction
- Waiting for a decision or event
- Demanding schedules, deadlines, time pressure, and having to clock in
- Too much responsibility
- Lack of freedom to express themselves and do things their way
- Lack of challenge or competition
- People who are too serious and rarely laugh
- Lack of fun, entertainment, and activities
- Inability to negotiate, change the outcome or bend the rules
- Pessimistic attitudes towards their ideas
- Being told how to work, what to do and when to do it
- A negative environment
- Repetition or routine work
- Theories, concepts, goal statements, and philosophies
- Requirement to follow detailed instructions or read manuals

A PROMOTER'S VALUE TO A TEAM

Promoters enjoy interacting and are good at influencing people. They are excellent at establishing and maintaining the social connections necessary for a team to function effectively. They can make even the mundane tasks fun.

A PROMOTER'S IDEAL ROLE IN A PROJECT

Promoters like to lead projects with their energy, innovation, and motivation. They are quick to seize opportunities and can persuade people to not only see the vision; but, take necessary actions to produce superior results. They are peak performers when faced with a challenge; and, if need be, can change direction with ease. They thrive on risk, multi-tasking, and finding solutions to a crisis. They are strategic and get things done in record time – performance is their strength.

HOW TO IMPROVE THE JOB PERFORMANCE OF A PROMOTER

- Give them an opportunity to take spontaneous action
- Allow for mobility and movement
- Understand their preference for action over words
- Give them tasks or projects that are action-packed and require a hands-on approach
- Provide opportunities for competition on the job
- Encourage them to use their flair and originality
- Come up with opportunities where they can be adventurous and skillful
- Utilize their natural negotiating abilities
- Allow them to share their excellent sense of humor
- Praise their skillfulness and performance on the job
- Give them the freedom to do their job using their non-traditional style

CHAPTER 15

APPRECIATING THE PLANNER AT WORK

Planners are the doers of the world and work slowly, steadily and diligently until the job is done. They pay particular attention to all the details along the way. When given a job to do, they work tirelessly to get it done in a timely fashion, ensuring that it's completed correctly the first time.

It is imperative to let them know expectations ahead of time, including required deadlines; otherwise, they get extremely stressed. Planners don't like surprises and they have a difficult time changing direction once they have started a job, so the more clearly you specify needs up front, the better results they will give.

The Planner personality style are not visionaries, but they are the ones that bring a vision to fruition, planning every required step to reach the goal. They are linear thinkers, gifted at seeing how one step leads to another. They tend to worry about what could go wrong and will spend time creating a detailed strategy that may include plan B, just in case. Planners are efficient, dependable and responsible and can be counted on to implement and execute any goal, ensuring there is no waste of time or money.

Planners are intelligent and are suited well for administrative or white-collar work. Their brains are concerned with order, control, and proper attention to detail. People admire them for their work ethic, devotion, and perseverance.

Because Planners are so dutiful, hardworking and task-oriented, they often end up in management roles. With ease, they bring order out of chaos and are exceptionally gifted at organizing and creating efficient systems.

Sticking to their well-designed plan is very important to Planners. They don't do well with quick change or change of direction unless they are told the reasons why change is necessary and have plenty of time to adjust their plan accordingly. Work always comes before play for Planners, which is the main reason others may sometimes perceive them as workaholics.

Because Planners always have a to-do list and an agenda, they tend to expect others to perform at the speed they do, which may leave people in their presence feeling hurried or rushed. They are very firm, direct and opinionated and typically present themselves as relatively serious folks, often offering little in regards to humor. If you disturb a Planner when they are focused on a task; they may seem impatient, harsh, blunt and insensitive; but, in their minds, they are just trying to do the work they had planned on.

Planners appear confident, speak succinctly and get to the point quickly. They always have an agenda, even at social gatherings. Following rules and policies are deemed as necessary to Planners and they are instrumental in creating them, if there are none in place.

Planner may experience unnecessary stress by not asking for help when they feel overwhelmed. They tend to take on too much work and then attempt to do it all themselves, to ensure that it will be done right. They may find it challenging, devoting time to training and mentoring others on how to do it correctly. Once they learn how to delegate and trust others though, they can work like a well-oiled machine, producing remarkable results.

A Planner's office is neat, tidy, orderly and clean. There will be a calendar and a clock visible. They don't like clutter, so decorations are minimal; maybe one or two family photos. Any artwork usually represents their traditional values and they may also have their licenses and certificates framed and posted. Policies and procedures, rules and safety guidelines will be on a bookshelf for quick reference. Planners dress in more formal attire. They are usually modest and coordinated. Their posture is erect and their mannerism is polite; they are respectful and always prepared.

Planners see punctuality as a sign of respect and do whatever it takes to honor their time obligations. They are impatient with people who are late and skip work for minor reasons. Due to their honesty and dedication, absenteeism from work is rare.

ON THE JOB, PLANNERS EXCEL AT

- Organizing people, projects or events
- Development of efficient systems
- Planning, including every detail required to achieve the goal
- Honesty and trust, being fair and just
- Knowing the rules, regulations, policies and procedures
- Supervising others to take correct action
- Accomplishing tasks, right and on time
- Self-motivation and discipline – they will work tirelessly to complete all their duties
- Making sound decisions, based on facts
- Saving time, money and resources

WORK FRUSTRATIONS AND STRESSORS FOR PLANNERS

- Change of plans, details, or method of doing something
- Policies and procedures that are incomplete or not clear
- Interruptions – feeling a lack of control
- Deadlines not met by others, or lack of follow-through
- Being surprised – not knowing what to expect
- Lack of management or leadership
- Carrying the workload of others – feeling people don't work as hard as they do
- Unclear expectations or direction for projects
- Small talk or conversations unrelated to work matters

- Tight or rushed deadlines - insufficient time to make a decision or complete a task
- Lack of planning, goals, focus or direction
- Details not being followed
- Mistakes and errors made by others
- An unorganized or cluttered atmosphere
- Wasted time, money or resources
- Inconsistencies
- Loud noises
- Lack of professionalism
- Meetings without a purpose
- Non-conformity to rules and directives
- Spontaneity, having to think on their feet or act quickly

A PLANNER'S VALUE TO A TEAM

Planners provide stability and maintain organization. They will take charge and are good at planning all the details while managing people and/or the project. They live by the clock and ensure things are complete on schedule. They maintain budgets. Planners are the worker bees.

A PLANNER'S IDEAL ROLE IN A PROJECT

Planner should be involved in the entire planning process. If the plan is already in place, let them know what their role is, how much responsibility is theirs and what your expectations are, including any deadlines. They will ensure a high level of production is maintained and will work hard to reach the expected standards, being sure that everything is done correctly and on time. Planners take initiative and make great project managers.

HOW TO IMPROVE THE JOB PERFORMANCE OF A PLANNER

- Assign tasks that require detailed planning and careful follow-through

- Give recognition and tangible rewards for a job well done
- Give clearly defined instructions and expectations
- Be punctual, reliable, and dependable
- Recognize their need for professionalism, direct communication, and responsible business practices
- Provide a structured, stable, and safe work environment, void of unforeseen changes
- On any project reassure them every step of the way that they are on the right track
- Praise their efficiency, neatness, and organizational abilities
- Provide, adhere to, and enforce rules and regulations
- Show good work ethics by sharing in the responsibilities and duties of the workplace

Chapter 16

Appreciating the Thinker at Work

Thinkers can be very academic and serious in their work environment. They are highly intelligent and love intellectual challenges in an atmosphere of rationality and freedom. Being gifted at conceptualizing things can make them an enormous contribution to any organization. Their preference is to deal with concepts and ideas rather than details, which they find tedious. They will however, pay particular attention to details when they are diagnosing, inventing, experimenting or working on projects that involve statistics and data. They are sticklers for accuracy and can be counted on to deliver excellent results.

Thinkers find their greatest joy and satisfaction when they are asked to develop models and strategies to move the organization forward. They love creating diagrams and charts, making projections, debating and discussing new ideas. They put thought into improving the way things are done and will work endlessly to achieve a goal, removing obstacles and solving problems that crop up along the way.

Although very competent, the depth of their knowledge often goes unnoticed by others; especially if they rarely display the dimensions of their personality in the workplace. Their lack of enthusiasm for organizational life and their quirky outward behavior can get falsely mistaken for incompetence by their co-workers and employers. Their strong desire to show their competency brings important programs and projects into being. Thinkers are driven and can be change agents on a global scale.

They most often converse about facts, histories, ideas or principles. Small talk at the coffee machine has little appeal. When exposed to small talk, they will likely zone out and entertain more important thoughts in their heads. They prefer their communication be concise, logical, and clearly expressed. Don't expect them to volunteer any personal disclosures. Some find their communication dry and have a difficult time understanding them, due to their use of technical jargon and abnormal phrases, with little display of emotion. For these reasons, people may feel intellectually inadequate in their presence and might avoid conversing with them unless necessary.

Thinkers are very deliberate, conscientious and methodical in the tasks they undertake and strive to be the best at everything they do. Data and analysis are paramount to them. They may get accused of being procrastinators, because things often take a long time to complete. Their approach to any problem is to take the time to gather information, then study and analyze the situation with all available resources to ensure there are no errors made. They rely heavily on data and facts and will ask the people involved for their experiences, yet are rarely influenced purely by human emotions.

Thinkers may be questioning, asking a lot of, "Why," and "How" questions. That's because they have an unquenchable desire for knowledge. Their brains are wired to want to know not only how things work but also why.

In the work environment, get them involved in technology issues, designing systems, or problems that need to be solved. Because they are perfectionists, they need to be given clear objectives and freedom, without time pressure, to be confident in their resolution. They usually prefer to work on projects independently, in a quiet place. Thinkers will respond favorably to people, when they receive acknowledgment for their valued contribution.

When additional insights and observations are necessary, ask a Thinker to participate. They consider it fun to pick ideas apart and put them back together again. Thinkers enjoy experimenting, developing a new approach, creating strategies for change, as well as designing systems, prototypes, and drafts. They rarely have reverence for long-standing traditions, because they are driven to improve on the status quo.

Thinkers will always question a new idea to ensure it can stand on its own merits. If an idea is not logical, consistent, verifiable, sensible, and sound, they will criticize it, no matter who the originating authority was. Thinkers are confident and self-assured, not easily swayed by status, titles or the opinions of others. They are only impressed by people who competently live up to the title bestowed on them. Likewise, the only meaningful compliments that a Thinker accepts are compliments about their ingenuity or intellect. Their self-esteem and confidence escalate when they discover new stand-alone ideas, not by unwarranted praise for tending to trivial tasks.

Thinkers are proficient with technology and they are also extremely useful at fixing technological issues. They are very patient and work tirelessly connecting all the dots until a technical issue is solved.

Thinkers love to research and spend countless hours devouring information on relevant or interesting topics. When a project requires research, ask them to participate and they will deliver excellent results.

A Thinker's office does not focus on creature comforts. Decorations are either useful or practical. They will have the latest technology and equipment. With the various projects they have underway, piles of paper will be in different places on topics they are researching. It may look chaotic; but Thinkers know where everything is and they don't want anyone to touch anything or try to organize their space. They will most definitely have a bookshelf filled with books, manuals and additional papers, all reflecting their interests in learning, diversity, innovation and new ideas.

Thinkers dress comfortable and informal. Their manner is mostly reserved and questioning. They prefer to be left alone to reflect and find solutions.

Thinkers always consider global impact when they undertake any major project. They are the world's innovators, helping to bring about advances to society, and adding to our understanding of the universe.

ON THE JOB, THINKERS EXCEL AT

- Generating ideas and solving problems
- Gathering information and data
- Innovation, doing what others say can't be done
- Being competent and proficient, thorough and accurate, tenacious and persistent
- Working on projects independently
- Evaluating and looking at all angles, to ensure their decision making is logical
- Identifying loopholes and closing them
- Creating a vision or "big picture"
- Having high standards; with precision they strive for perfection
- Critiquing and testing ideas, systems, theories, etc.
- Being up-to-date on how to use or fix modern technology
- Creating systems and graphs
- Grammar; they know the correct usage, meaning, and spelling of complicated words
- Objectively, they are able to hold their ground, without feeling threatened or swayed

WORK FRUSTRATIONS FOR THINKERS

- Incompetence
- Being given a project or goal without clear objectives - generalization, no clarity or specifics
- Pressure to perform tasks within a particular time frame
- Lack of systems
- Unfairness
- Technological failures
- Not being able to question something or someone
- Being asked to do something illogical
- Distractions and noise that interrupts their thinking process
- Ignorance, careless mistakes, and errors

- Not enough time to gather facts and data before making decisions
- Poor grammar or spelling
- Lack of mental challenges or lack of freedom
- Small talk or emotional outbursts
- Being cornered or pressured for immediate answers, or feeling boxed-in
- Unproductive meetings
- Having to work on a project with others who don't share their thinking
- Submitting to an authority that they find incompetent
- Having to adhere to rules, policies and procedures that they deem as useless

A THINKER'S VALUE TO A TEAM

Thinkers bring about improvements and solve complex problems. They are inventive, conceptual and objective. Developing models, exploring ideas and building systems satisfies their need to be innovative. They are perfect for research, analysis, and understanding technology and its functions.

A THINKER'S IDEAL ROLE IN A PROJECT

Give Thinkers the responsibility of helping formulate and analyze the objectives of the project, to ensure you have sufficient supporting data and logic before proceeding. They will work to go beyond the status quo, charting a new course and setting records, or doing what no one before them has ever done. They are global thinkers and always look for ways of improving things. Thinkers will work tirelessly to ensure the project is error-free and successful.

HOW TO IMPROVE THE JOB PERFORMANCE OF A THINKER

- Allow them to have autonomy in their work
- Designate projects to them that require problem-solving and analytical thinking

- Recognize and appreciate their competence on the job
- Give them free reign to improve systems
- Encourage independent thinking to advance their ideas
- Ask them to share their vision and what global impact it may have
- Inspire them with futuristic ideas and possible improvements
- Respect their need to avoid redundancy and repetitive tasks
- Praise their innovation, inventiveness, and ingenuity
- Respect their tendency to go beyond the established rules of the system

PART VI

Living A Purposeful Life

"Life is a miracle. YOU are a unique expression of this purposeful
miracle. Think of how GREAT that makes you. Live big!
You are not here to dwell within the basement of your potentiality."
Dr. Steve Maraboli

CHAPTER 17

PASSION IS THE COMPASS TO YOUR PURPOSE

YOUR LIFE MATTERS

- Are you living up to your potential?
- Do you feel unfulfilled and unsatisfied?
- Do fear and uncertainty bind you?
- Does life seem meaningless and empty?
- Do you know your life's purpose?

If you are stirred by the above questions or feel that your life is lacking in meaning, the next two chapters are designed to help you discover your passion and purpose so you can live the life you were meant to live.

You were born with everything needed to fulfill your calling and purpose. You have the desire, ability, and you heart is filled with passion. You've been equipped you with the required gifts, ideas, creativity, and specific areas in which you will shine. No dream is too big; no challenge is too great.

We keep trying to fix things in ourselves that are not broken. We need to stop comparing ourselves with others, trying to turn ourselves into the best version of somebody else. We have been created the way we are, with the gifts we have, to fulfill our destiny.

Aim for a life worth living by expressing the passion in your heart. People who live passionate lives are contagious!

PASSION = PURPOSE

GREEK: Passion is a feeling of intense enthusiasm (entheos) which means "filled with God."

Passion is God within; it is the compass to our purpose. Our passion is our purpose!

QUALITIES TO HELP US IDENTIFY OUR PURPOSE

If we are passionate and enthusiastic about an issue or need in the world that we can't let go of or that we daydream about changing, it's a sign that you are being steered towards your purpose. When something is our passion, we can't get enough of it. We read about it, study it, and never run out of ideas about it.

Below are some common qualities people have when they are identifying their passion:

- We have a vision (passion) of how an issue or need in the world could be different. This stirring, thought, dream, feeling, prompting or wish won't leave us alone. We can't dismiss it because it shows up again and again in our mind.
- The need (pain or frustration with what is) in our vision, tugs at our heart. We may see things on TV or in our community that instantly stir up pain and frustration for us, and we wish we could do something to change it.
- We desire to pursue our vision to serve others. It feels like it's our assignment.
- Ease, flow, and great joy accompany any work we do that resembles our vision/dream.
- We resist our vision because it feels too big, may upset current plans, is daunting, scary or inconvenient. Consider it may just be exactly what we should do.

- We don't have everything we need to pursue the vision. We justify that we can't do it because we don't have the right relationships, skills or resources required. Trust that we will gather those things as we take a step of faith, not before.
- We are not yet who we need to be to complete our vision. We talk ourselves out of our calling by saying we lack the right education, charisma, courage, etc. to do it. Our callings are there to grow us. Step out in faith.

OUT OF PAIN, BEAUTY IS BORN

Our passion often comes from the painful events and trials we've endured in life. When we go through a hurt, we have first-hand experience and understanding, and develop empathy for others going through similar situations. Our suffering helps us grow by cultivating discipline, patience, and endurance in us. Often our pain reveals the purpose for our lives. Our mess often becomes our message.

Chapter 18

Discovering Your Purpose

DISCOVERING YOUR PURPOSE EXERCISE

To help you clarify and identify your purpose, spend some time reflecting on the following questions before you answer them. Some people find it helpful to journal about each question to achieve clarity.

1. When in your life have you been the happiest? (as a child and as an adult)

2. What activities were your favorite in the past? What about now?

3. What activities make you lose track of time?

4. What have you done that made you truly proud of yourself?

5. What is it that makes you feel alive, energized, and fulfilled?

6. Who inspires you and what qualities do they possess? (family, friends, authors, artists, leaders, etc. You may or may not know them personally)

7. What are you naturally good at? (skills, abilities, gifts, etc.)

8. What do people typically ask you for help with?

9. If you could teach anything you wanted, what would you teach?

10. What causes do you strongly connect with and believe in?

11. If you could relay a message that you're passionate about to a large audience, what would your message be and who would be in attendance listening?

12. If you could change or remove one thing in the world, what would it be? What would you replace it with? (Example: remove war and replace with peace, remove abuse and replace with total acceptance and love, remove poverty and replace with abundance).

PREPARING YOUR PURPOSE STATEMENT

When you have answered the above questions, prepare your life purpose statement by incorporating:

- Your personality/top gifts
- Your passion/purpose

Once you have identified your personality style, your passion, and purpose, draw a picture of your future or create a collage and write your purpose statement on it. Read it on a consistent basis to remind yourself of who you were created to be. I call it my 'Rule of Life' statement. Each time I'm presented with an opportunity I carefully assess it based on my gifts, passion, and purpose to see if it aligns with the core value of who I am. It acts as a compass to my best life.

PROVISION COMES AFTER WE STEP OUT IN FAITH

Taking the first step to follow our passion by serving others can be daunting, and downright scary. Reach deep within for faith, take a step and watch your doubts dissipate, your insecurities and fears vanish. When you're on the right track following your passion and purpose, you'll find open doors of opportunity. People will show up that can help you on your way.

PART VII

Showing Kindness

"You have not lived today until you have done something
for someone who can never repay you."
John Bunyan

Chapter 19

Making a Difference

PRACTICAL WAYS TO SERVE OTHERS

It feels good to make a difference in someone's life using your innate gifting; it's the only way to experience true passion, purpose, and joy!

You may be eager to make a difference but wonder where to start. Let your passion and purpose be your guide. Do some exploring of problems and issues in your community, maybe search for non-profit organizations where you can help, or consider starting with some of the suggestions listed below:

- Help a single mom feel refreshed by taking her kids for a few hours
- Help a widow with her yard work or necessary repairs
- Befriend a war veteran or someone with a disability
- Bring dinner to a family who has suffered a recent tragedy
- Visit the elderly and consider taking them out into nature or for ice cream
- Bring groceries to a family in need or give them a food voucher
- Help at a local food bank or donate food to them
- Send a care package or a letter to overseas troops
- Help a senior or a single parent organize their house
- Help an elderly person with house cleaning
- Run errands for the elderly
- Pray with someone who has a need
- Spend time with a struggling teenager and do something fun with them

- Buy an outfit for a single mom
- Offer a ride to someone who has no car
- Make care packages to hand out to people asking for money
- Befriend an elderly person who is lonely – there is a great need in this area as many are lonely, especially those who live alone
- Donate clothes
- Get to know your neighbor by having them over for a meal
- Throw a birthday party for a child in an impoverished neighborhood
- Buy school supplies for a low-income family
- Bring food and beverages to a single person who is too sick to get out
- Bring flowers from your garden to someone who is sick or elderly
- Take someone's pet for a walk if they are ill or unable to do it themselves

If you have time for a greater commitment, consider these ideas:

- Raise funds for a cause you strongly believe in and connect with
- Become a mentor
- Hold a neighborhood food drive
- Arrange a team to help clean up your community, or a park
- Volunteer at a soup kitchen, a shelter for the homeless, youth center, etc.
- Share produce from your garden or fruit trees
- Prepare meals for an elderly person living alone
- Volunteer for Hospice, or visit people in jail, a nursing home, or hospital
- Donate your skills as a plumber, electrician, handyman, mechanic, hairstylist, etc. to help someone who can't afford to hire help
- Adopt a foster child to keep them out of the human trafficking circle
- Become an honorary aunt or uncle to a foster child
- Hold a neighborhood coat drive in the early winter months
- Arrange fun activities for children of impoverished families
- Create an organization to fill a need
- Gather blankets from neighbors and deliver them to the homeless
- Teach free classes to youths like; photography, flower arranging, woodworking, mechanics, painting, drawing, cooking, outdoor survival, sewing, music, gardening, graphic design, etc.
- Start a movement that will have a positive impact in your community; like 'pay it forward,' 'random acts of kindness,' etc.

- Go on a mission trip to build homes for the less fortunate
- Start a coffee house with live music in your neighborhood where new residents or lonely people can gather to have fellowship

The possibilities are endless. It starts with every person looking into their hearts to see what calls to them; getting in touch with their passion and taking action to make a difference. Find a need and fill it. When you open yourself up to serving by using your gifts, you'll be surprised at how many opportunities will show up.

PART VIII

Reflection

"Life is truly reflection of what we
allow ourselves to see and be."
Trudy Symeonakis Vesotsky

Chapter 20

You Are Uniquely Designed

Take time to outline and reflect on the unique way you are designed.

- I am an: Extrovert/Introvert (Covered in Chapter 3)

    Add a check mark next to how you best restore your energy below.

    My energy is restored when I am:

    1. _____ with people, or

    2. _____ alone

- My personality style ranking is: (Covered in Chapter 4)

    1. _____ Dominant Style

    2. _____ Secondary Backup Style

    3. _____ Third Style

    4. _____ Challenging Style

- My purpose statement is: (Covered in Chapter 18)

    _____

    _____

    _____

    _____

- My next step to living out loud – A life of passion, purpose, and joy is:

_____

_____

_____

_____

Chapter 21

Ways to Live Out Loud

LOVE THEM ANYWAY BY MOTHER TERESA

1. People are often unreasonable, irrational, and self-centered. Forgive them anyway.
2. If you are kind, people may accuse you of selfish, ulterior motives. Be kind anyway.
3. If you are successful, you will win some unfaithful friends and some genuine enemies. Succeed anyway.
4. If you are honest and sincere people may deceive you. Be honest and sincere anyway.
5. What you spend years creating, others could destroy overnight. Create anyway.
6. If you find serenity and happiness, some may be jealous. Be happy anyway.
7. The good you do today, will often be forgotten. Do good anyway.
8. Give the best you have, and it will never be enough. Give your best anyway.
9. In the final analysis, it is between you and God. It was never between you and them anyway.

ABOUT THE AUTHOR

Erika Larsson is passionate about helping people identify their natural gifts so they can maximize their potential, clarify their purpose, and live a meaningful and fulfilling life of passion and joy.

She brings energy and enthusiasm to her writing, speaking, and training interactions. Erika has designed workshops since 1990 and has spoken to audiences as large as 3,000 people. For 25 years, she has been a personality-style enthusiast and attributes her personal and professional success to understanding the four personality temperaments that we interact with in our day-to-day activities.

Erika continues to lead a business career that has seen noteworthy success in the fields of marketing, training, speaking, sales, service, and education, producing superior results in whatever she undertakes. Her innovative efforts have resulted in numerous professional accolades and extensive positive coverage both on TV and in the press. She was nominated for the YMCA's "Woman of Distinction" award in the category of Entrepreneur/Innovator. She also designed a women's mentorship program that received recognition from the British Columbia Provincial Government in Canada.

Erika was born in Norway and immigrated to Canada at age eleven with her family. In 2015 she immigrated to the US and has settled just north of Seattle, Washington where she continues her practice of providing training in personality temperaments to both small and large audiences.

Her goal is to challenge, inspire and motivate people to understand themselves and others so they can create lasting relationships based on total acceptance and mutual respect. Her mission is to share her knowledge and expertise with people who want to take their life to the next level so they can live out loud.

You can find information about Erika's training seminars, speaking, video blog, and books at:

www.ErikaLarsson.com

SEMINARS AND TESTIMONIALS

If you desire a deeper understanding of yourself and others in your personal or professional life attend or host one of her many seminars outlined at:

www.ErikaLarsson.com

TESTIMONIALS

"I went to the workshop for fun and to gain pointers that I could use in business. Erika's teaching delivered more than expected; it was so practical that I use what I learned on a daily basis. Her teaching helped me gain a deeper understanding of myself and the behavioral traits of the different personality types, resulting in better relationships with my family, coworkers, and spouse. I'm able to appreciate our differences and can see the contribution that each one brings to my world. By understanding the people that I interact with, I'm better able to navigate through life without all the speedbumps."
Lynn Wise, CFO of Cement Distributors Inc.

"She is a highly skilled seminar and workshop leader. She leaves her audience motivated and eager to put what they have learned into practice."
Matti Anttila, Author, Seminar Leader, Entrepreneur

"Erika has the distinct ability to target the strengths, and areas for growth, of all the individuals she interacts with. She has the skills and training to engage audiences small or large and leaves them with the tools and encouragement to grow in their business and personal lives. Any company that has the opportunity to work with Erika will experience a true professional and team leader."
Bill MacMunn, Triple Diamond Global Expansion Leader with Valentus

"Erika has not only helped me interact with my clients and colleagues but with my friends and family. I never knew much about the four personality styles prior to meeting her. It has taught me a lot about my own personality and that of others. I am pleased to have this knowledge and feel better equipped to help my clients and loved ones by paying closer attention to their needs. Thank you, Erika, for sharing this knowledge in such a clear and concise way."
Stephanie Prest, Artist

"We were lucky enough to have Erika come into our company to provide training on the four personality styles! Right away we gained a deeper understanding of one another, and the different working styles we have. Understanding our strengths and weaknesses has helped us work better as a team. I would highly recommend any small (or large) business owner invest in this training! It has helped us build a more cohesive team."

Shawna Talley – Loan Officer, Network Home Loans

"Erika helped me clarify my gifts. I've been able to use the information I learned to launch myself out of "stuck mode." My new level of clarity helps me to see myself and others in a positive light, giving me a newfound boldness to use my gifts to live the life I was created to live. Erika's encouragement will inspire you to become all that God meant for you to be. I owe some of my most recent success to the wisdom I've gained from Erika's teachings."

Jen Hylton, Wellness Advocate

"Erika is passionate about this topic and is truly inspiring in sharing a much-needed seminar on gifting and purpose."

Dianne L. Thomsen, Healthy Lifestyle Coach

"Erika is a hard-working entrepreneurial individual who has an incredible talent for understanding human behavior. It's a pleasure to work with someone with such vast experience. If you get the pleasure of working with her, I'd highly recommend it. A top performer in all aspects!

Earl Flormata, Chief Marketing Officer at Mind of a Marketer

ERIKA'S BOOKS

Erika's books can be ordered on Amazon.com, www.ErikaLarsson.com or emailing admin@ErikaLarsson.com

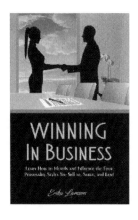

WINNING IN BUSINESS - Learn How to Identify and Influence the Four Personality Styles You Sell To, Serve, and Lead ($20.00 + shipping and handling)

"If you are looking to understand how to serve your customers at an even higher level in ways you likely have never considered, get Erika's book, *WINNING IN BUSINESS - Learn How to Identify and Influence the Four Personality Styles You Sell To, Serve, and Lead.* It offers insights from a potent personality perspective that helps you earn credibility, build trust, and establish loyal business relationships. Erika offers her expertise and observations from over 25 years of experience in the field of customer service with her easy-to-read, straightforward, spirited writing style. You'll learn about yourself, your colleagues, and your competition as well as your customers in this valuable book."

Mary Miscisin, Author of Personality Lingo and Showing Our True Colors, Noted Speaker

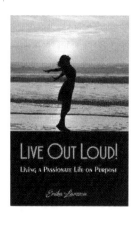

LIVE OUT Loud! Living a Passionate Life on Purpose ($20.00 + shipping and handling)

"Erika's book, *LIVE OUT LOUD! Living a Passionate Life on Purpose,* provides amazing insight into four personality styles that will give you a better understanding of any person in your life. It will surely improve your relationships and interactions with others. Learn how to avoid misunderstandings and improve your communication skills."

Marilyn Anderson, BGS, B.Ed., and Language Skills Instructor

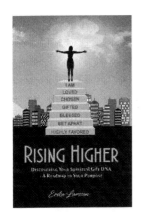

Rising Higher - Discovering Your Spiritual Gift DNA – A Roadmap to Your Purpose ($20.00 + shipping and handling)

"Have you ever wondered what you should do with your life in the midst of the many options and choices you have? Erika's *RISING HIGHER – Discovering Your Spiritual Gift DNA – A Roadmap to Your Purpose* book will help you with that decision by providing insights into how God has designed you. Questions such as what excites you, what gets your imagination going, what gives you a sense of purpose, and what makes you come alive are green lights in the decision-making process. I highly encourage you to spend some time with her book and the insights she brings to the process. You will be a more fulfilled and blessed person for doing so and thus, a greater blessing to others and the Kingdom of God."

Keith Hook, Mission Leader/Former Missionary and Pastor

REFERENCES

Erika Larsson ©2018 *Rising Higher – Discovering Your Spiritual Gift DNA – A Roadmap to Your Purpose*
Kindle Direct Publishing, North Charleston, South Carolina

Erika Larsson ©2017 *Winning in Business – Learn How to Identify and Influence the Four Personality Styles You Sell To, Serve, and Lead*
Kindle Direct Publishing, North Charleston, South Carolina

Jessica Butts ©2015 *Live Your Life from the Front Seat – Accomplishing Magnificent Things in Your Life, Relationships and Career*
Legacy One Authors, Kirkland, Washington

Mary Miscisin ©2014 *Personality Lingo*
Kindle Direct Publishing, North Charleston, South Carolina

Ann Kashiwa ©2011 *Meaningful Conversations – Connecting the DOT and True Colors*
True Colors Int., Santa Ana, California

Michael J. Losier ©2009 *Law of Connection – The Science of Using NLP to Create Ideal Personal and Professional Relationships*
Wellness Central – Hatchette Book Group, New York, New York

Mary Miscisin ©2005 *Showing Our True Colors*
True Colors Inc., Santa Ana, California

Kathy Hayward ©2005 *True Parenting – How to Foster Deeper Family Ties and a Harmonious Home*
True Colors Inc. Publishing, Santa Ana, California

Dani Johnson ©2005 *Gems Introductory – Instantly Detect & Influence Personality Types with Ease*
Legacy Media, LTD. Published by Call to Freedom Int'l, LLC.

Carolyn Kalil ©2000 *Follow Your True Colors to the Work You Love*
Bookpartners Inc., Wilsonville, Oregon

50452528R00087

Made in the USA
Columbia, SC
07 February 2019